Online Safety

The Complete Guide to Being Safe Online

Joe Malacina

Online Safety: The Complete Guide to Being Safe Online

Trademarks & Acknowledgements

author are not associated with any product or vendor mentioned in this book with the exception of Infinity Guides. *Online Safety: The Complete Guide to Being Safe Online* is an independent publication and has not been authorized, sponsored, or otherwise approved by any of the trademark or copyright owners referenced in this text.

Warning & Disclaimer

Every effort has been made to ensure this text is as accurate and complete as possible. This text does not cover every single aspect, nor was it intended to do so. Instead, the text is meant to be a building block for successful learning of the subject matter of this text. No warranty whatsoever is implied. The author and No Limit Enterprises, Inc. shall have neither liability nor responsibility to any person or entity with respect to any losses or damages arising from the information contained in this text.

Contact the Publisher

To contact No Limit Enterprises, Inc. or the author for sales, marketing material, or any commercial purpose, please visit www.nolimitcorp.com, or e-mail info@nolimitcorp.com.

Online Safety: The Complete Guide to Being Safe Online

Author: Joe Malacina

Publisher: No Limit Enterprises, Inc.

Cover Art by: Erik Christian Voigt

Print ISBN: 978-1-7342604-0-3

Electronic Book ISBN: 978-1-7342604-1-0

Library of Congress Control Number: 2019954575

Printed in the U.S.A.

About the Author

Joe Malacina is the founder of *InfinityGuides.com*, a beginner's help website that offers books, DVDs, and online courses to help people learn how to use technology. Since 2013, *InfinityGuides.com* has taught over 100,000 people how to use their devices, social media, and today's consumer technology. Prior to authoring numerous how-to books, Malacina operated two popular tech blogs with a combined audience of over one million people that focused on the most popular smartphones and tablets. He has also been a guest speaker at technology and adult education conferences around the United States. His approach for teaching technology devices has focused on stressing the basics to build technological intuition, thus allowing users to become experts at using their devices in a relatively short amount of time. Following the success of his blogs and seminars, Malacina authored his first book, the *iPhone Manual for Beginners (1ˢᵗ Edition),* which was published in 2017 and reached the *InfinityGuides.com's* Best-Seller list within the first week, and remained there for over six months. His published works have earned praise from notable tech aficionados, adult and senior organizations, and readers alike, and can be found in households across the United States, Canada, Australia, and the United Kingdom.

Malacina holds an MBA in Finance from the University of Illinois at Chicago, and holds a Bachelor of Science in Mechanical Engineering from the same university. He has been profiled and interviewed on numerous radio stations, podcasts, and blogs and is often on a speaking tour in the United States and Canada. He lives and works in Chicago, IL, United States.

www.joemalacina.com

Also by Joe Malacina

iPhone Manual for Beginners: The Perfect iPhone Guide for Seniors, Beginners, & First-time iPhone Users

iPad Manual for Beginners: The Perfect iPad Guide for Beginners, Seniors, & First-time iPad Users

Galaxy S8 Manual for Beginners: The Perfect Galaxy S8 Guide for Beginners, Seniors, & First-time Galaxy Users

Kindle Manual for Beginners: The Perfect Kindle Guide for Beginners, Seniors, & First-time Kindle Users

Fire HD Manual for Beginners: The Complete Guide to using the Fire HD for Beginners, Seniors, & First-time Fire Tablet Users

Table of Contents

Introduction 11

Chapter 1 – Online Safety Basics 13

    Key Terms 13

    What to Expect 14

    How to Read This Book 14

Chapter 2 – Web Browsing Safety 15

    Choose Your Web Browser 15

    General Privacy Concerns 16

    Advertisements 19

    Ad Blockers 20

    A Final Note on Ads 21

    Referral Content 21

    Sponsored Content 24

    Fake News 27

    Clickbait 28

    Sharing your Personal Information 29

Chapter 3 – Online Shopping Safety 33

    The 1st Rule: SSL Security 33

    Paying for Online Purchases 35

    The 2nd Rule: Never Use a Debit Card, Electronic Check, or Bank (ACH) Transfer to Pay Online 36

    Third-Party Payers 37

    Online Receipts 38

    Trusting Websites 38

    Online Shopping Tips 40

Chapter 4 – Email Safety 41

    Built-In Safety 41

    Spam & Junk Mail 41

    Phishing Emails 47

    Checking Links in Email Messages 50

Email Attachments 52

Common Fraudulent Emails 53

Never Trust a Name 56

More Email Best Practices 57

Chapter 5 – Social Media Safety 61

The #1 Rule of Social Media 61

Internet Trolls 63

Facebook Safety 64

Facebook: Common Scams 64

Facebook: Friends & Friend Requests 66

Facebook: Private Messages 67

Facebook: Best Practices 67

Twitter Safety 75

Twitter: Warnings 75

Twitter: Following & Followers 75

Twitter: Direct Messages 76

Twitter: Tweets & Links 76

Twitter: Common Scams 77

Twitter: Safety Features 78

Twitter: Best Practices 80

Instagram Safety 80

Instagram: Your Profile, Followers, & Following 81

Instagram: Direct Messages 82

Instagram: Safety Features 82

Instagram: Best Practices 83

Snapchat Safety 83

Snapchat: Warnings 84

Snapchat: Friends 85

Snapchat: Private Messages 85

Snapchat: Risks 86

Snapchat: Best Practices 86

General Best Practices of Social Media.. 87

Chapter 6 – Mobile Device Safety.. 89

Safety of Different Brands... 89

Mobile Web Browsing.. 91

Texting & Messaging Safety 92

Phone Call Scams & Telemarketing.. 99

Mobile Phone Privacy.. 101

Chapter 7 – Computer Safety 107

Windows PC vs. Mac vs Others 107

Types of Malicious Software & Nomenclature 108

Virus Protection Software 109

Keep Your Computer Up to Date 110

Backing up your Data 110

More Safety Tips for your Computer 111

Recommended Software and Apps.. 112

Chapter 8 – Online Dating Safety... 113

Online Dating Platforms 113

Protecting Yourself... 114

Investigating and Verifying Other Users 116

Meeting someone you met Online 117

Chapter 9 – Online Safety for Parents with Children................................. 119

Education: The First Step is the #1 Rule of Social Media 119

Education: Know what your Children are using... 120

Education: Social Media Risks 121

Education: Other Online Risks for Children 125

Prevention: Parental Controls... 125

Prevention: Financial Data for your Child 139

Prevention: Built-in Tools... 140

Best Practices 140

Acronyms Commonly Used by Teens... 142

Chapter 10 – What to do when you're a Victim 143

Minimize the Damage 143

Example 1: Credit Card Details Stolen... 146

Example 2: Online Password Stolen.. 147

Fortify your Defenses 148

Chapter 11 – Tips & Tricks 149

Online Password Safety... 149

Craigslist Safety 155

Online Jargon.. 160

Off The Grid 161

Chapter 12 – Conclusion & More Resources 167

More Resources 167

Appendix A – Common Online Acronyms.. 169

Appendix B – List of Best Practices 171

Introduction

Congratulations! So you have decided to embark on the important aspect of online safety. This book will be your most essential tool in protecting yourself and others from the substantial dangers of using the internet. I wanted to take this time to tell you how this book is going to be your vital resource for navigating the digital world. You see, the internet is not what it used to be. In the past, the internet was confined to surfing the web or sending an email on a computer. Today, the internet is everywhere, always on, and always affecting our lives. In other words, it is inescapable. Naturally, with the expansion of the internet has come the increase of diverse scams, fraud, and other digital threats.

According to the United States Federal Bureau of Investigation's Internet Crime Report, in 2017 there were 300,000 complaints related to internet crime in the United States with a total monetary loss of over $1.4 billion. The statistics reported in this report were staggering and showed that threats on the internet are increasing each and every year, with scammers increasingly making use of social media, email, and mobile devices. Furthermore, the report showed that people over the age of 60 were most likely to be targeted and suffered the most financial losses.

This report by for the FBI gives a small glimpse of the reality of how the expansion of the internet has certainly led to the expansion of online scams and fraud. Unfortunately, nobody is immune to being targeted online, and this includes people of all ages and of all locations throughout the world. The 300,000 complaints reported may seem like a relatively low number for the United States, however it is worth noting that the FBI also estimated that up to 90% of all cybercrimes go unreported.

Despite these harrowing statistics, don't let the fear of using the internet and its accompanying devices prevent you from embracing the digital world and exploring all it has to offer. This book will show you how to use the internet safely in most situations, and will give you the tools to protect yourself from just about any online threat. Most importantly, this book will educate you on exactly what to look out for when using the internet. By just being educated on the basics of online safety and following my **best practices**, you will be able to use the internet on all of your devices freely without having to agonize about a scam or online predator.

This book is structured so that you can go to any chapter at any time and learn exactly what you need. I do recommend that you read the first couple chapters however, as they will explain some important aspects of online safety that everyone should know. Furthermore, if you have read any of my books in the past you will know that all of my books, including this one, teach from the perspective of a beginner. In other words, if you have never used the internet, a smartphone, or social media before; that will be no detriment when reading this book. On the flipside, seasoned internet users should find this book very helpful as well, as the trends in online safety have changed greatly over the years. No matter what your skill or experience level, the information contained in this text will educate you and improve your ability to use the internet safely.

Lastly, you may be wondering where all of this information about online safety comes from, and if it will be relevant to you. You also may be wondering if you need this book, or if it will answer all of your questions. I can assure you that the information addressed in this book is derived directly from the input of hundreds of thousands of people who have had the same questions and concerns as you. I have been teaching people of all ages and backgrounds how to use the internet, social media, and technology devices professionally since 2013. Through this, I have been asked tens of thousands of questions about various aspects of online safety. So I can assure you, I know what the most common questions are and where the most concern lies, and this book will address them.

On a final note, I do recommend that you keep this book handy in your home or office after you have finished reading it. Undoubtedly, there will come a time when you need to refer to it again and the Table of Contents or Index can quickly lead you to your answer. Furthermore, for the best experience I also recommend that you read this entire book instead of just skipping through to specific chapters. It may not seem like it, but just about every aspect of online safety is interlinked, and having a good comprehension of each aspect will be beneficial to you when using the internet. Finally, I cannot stress enough how important the **Best Practices** in this book are. These practices are tried, true, and tested when it comes it online safety, and they will aid you in having the safest online experience.

On that introduction, let us get started.

Chapter 1 – Online Safety Basics

So what exactly is online safety anyways? Many people think online safety is protecting your financial information online when making purchases. Others believe online safety is protecting yourself from scammers who are trying to take your money or protecting your children from predators on social media. All of these are great examples of online safety, but are just a drop in the bucket of what truly entails the definition. For this book, we will define online safety as utilizing the tools, knowledge, and best practices of this book to use technology and the internet as you specifically intend, without causing harm to you or others. In layman's terms, this definition means online safety is using technology and the internet exactly as you want, without falling victim to negative consequences.

Before I show you how to be safe online, let's familiarize ourselves with some key terms that I will use often in this book. These terms are important for you to remember, as you will encounter them often.

Key Terms

<u>Online</u> – Being connected to the internet, generally through a device such as a smartphone, computer, or tablet.

<u>Best Practice</u> – A method, rule, or practice you can follow that will typically provide the best result. All Best Practices in this book will be noted and I highly recommend following them.

<u>Social Media</u> – Any online or digital platform where it's main purpose is to connect people together digitally in a social setting. Examples of social media include: Facebook, Twitter, Instagram, Snapchat, and Pinterest.

<u>Smartphone</u> – A smartphone is an electronic cellular phone that can do additional tasks besides phone calls and text messaging. Two examples of smartphones are the Apple iPhone and Samsung Galaxy.

<u>Tablet</u> – A tablet is an electronic device similar to a smartphone that can do various online tasks such as surf the web and use email. Examples of tablets include the Apple iPad and the Samsung Galaxy Tab.

Digital World – The digital world is an all-encompassing term that describes the internet and the many ways we use it, including through computers, smartphones, tablets, and social media.

What to Expect

Many people expect when picking up this book that they are going to be overloaded with doom and gloom scenarios, and that this book will attempt to frighten you into never turning your smartphone or computer on again unless you want to be victimized. That is not the case whatsoever! Instead, this book will educate you on what exactly is out there, and what you can do to have the best and safest experience online. By simply knowing what the risks are, you can easily prevent yourself from becoming a victim. Furthermore, this book will demonstrate proven techniques and best practices for online safety, that when employed significantly prevent the chance of harm coming to yourself online.

How to Read This Book

If you have read through the introduction, then you already know that I stated you can read this book in any way that you wish. My personal recommendation is that you read the book from cover to cover, and skip over any sections or chapters that you are absolutely sure will have no value to you. For instance, if you do not have dependent children then you can completely skip Chapter 9, which covers how to keep your kids safe online. I also recommend when reading that you pay special attention to the best practices that are listed in each chapter, as these are the most important tidbits of information that you will come across. Once you have finished reading this book, you should keep the book in your possession and refer to it when you come across a particular situation online. For example, if you receive an email that is suspicious and are unsure what to do, you can open this book to Chapter 4 – Email Safety, and follow the recommendations to help you handle the email properly. Lastly, when reading this book try to keep in mind that the internet is mostly filled with great things that can make your life a lot easier and more enjoyable. It can be easy to lose sight of this as we cover many of the nefarious and unfortunate aspects of the digital world.

Chapter 2 – Web Browsing Safety

Web browsing is the act of visiting websites online, and using those websites for your purposes. We will start with web browsing safety first since it is one of the most fundamental aspects of the web, and has been around since the good old days of dialup internet. There are several safety components worth considering, and we will explore them in this chapter.

Choose Your Web Browser

Your web browser is simply the software or app you use to visit web pages and surf the internet. Most people do not put a lot of thought into which web browser they use, but you definitely should. Different web browsers have different features and characteristics, so choose a web browser that best works for your lifestyle.

> **Best Practice** – When deciding on a web browser, use one of the major and trusted browsers listed below. These browsers are reliable, secure, and are compatible with nearly every website. Furthermore, whichever web browser you choose, use that same browser across all of your devices if you can.

List of Trusted Web Browsers

- **Microsoft Edge** – This web browser is and has been considered the standard web browser for many years (its precursor was Internet Explorer). It is available on PCs and mobile devices, and is a very safe and reliable web browser.
- **Safari** – Safari is the web browser made by Apple, Inc, and comes preloaded on all Macs, iPhones, and iPads. It is also a very safe and reliable web browser. If you are an exclusive user of Apple products for your computers and mobile devices, using Safari as your web browser is a great option.
- **Mozilla Firefox** – Firefox is a web browser that generally does not come preloaded on any computer or device, and is immensely popular. The browser is reliable and safe, and has many options you can customize.
- **Chrome** – Chrome is the web browser made by Google, and comes preloaded on Chromebooks and many Android mobile devices. Chrome is one of the most popular web browsers as it is highly integrated with your Google account. If you use a lot of Google services and products, then using Chrome as your web browser is a great option.

- **Brave** – Brave is a fairly new and unique web browser that focuses completely on privacy. One of the best features of Brave is it blocks all ads on all web pages by default. Not only this, but Brave does not explicitly track your website behavior to better protect your privacy. If privacy is your main concern when browsing online, then I would recommend you use the Brave browser

Any of these web browsers are suitable for a safe and reliable internet browsing experience. They are all available online through a web search and most are available in your smartphone or tablet's app marketplace.

General Privacy Concerns

The first thing you need to understand is that when you are visiting websites on the internet, you can expect nearly every website to collect certain information from you, whether you consent to it or not. The type of information they collect is generally not personally identifiable, but is unnerving nonetheless, and is commonly referred to as cookies. It is difficult to avoid this data collection, as websites use the data to learn how visitors are interacting with their website, as well as how to best direct you to advertisements. The type of data they collect can include your: general location (such as city or town), web browser, device, basic demographic information, interests, and browsing history. This may seem a little invasive, and it is, but keep in mind that most of the data that these websites collect is aggregated, so they generally cannot see specific information about you. Moreover, many of these websites share this information with other entities. Let me give you an example to demonstrate exactly how this works, and you have probably noticed this yourself. If I were to go online and start visiting websites related to barbecue grills, and then subsequently logged in to my Facebook account; there is a good chance I would see advertisements on my Facebook feed for barbecue grills! This is exactly how data collection and sharing works among websites, and it is beneficial to be aware of this when browsing the internet.

Now what if you do not want your website activity collected and shared? There are things you can do to easily prevent this. Just about every browser has a mode you can enable called private browsing. When you are using private browsing, your internet browser will prevent websites from collecting certain data from you and sharing it. Furthermore, your web browser itself will not track your history or any activity you do while browsing.

Here is how you can enable private browsing on various web browsers. Please note private browsing is available on both desktop and mobile devices.

Microsoft Edge: Click on the <u>three horizontal dots</u> at the upper right hand corner, and then click on <u>New InPrivate Window</u>. (<u>Figure 2.1</u>)

<u>Figure 2.1</u> – Microsoft Edge Web Browser -> InPrivate Browsing

Chrome: Click on the <u>three horizontal dots</u> at the upper right hand corner, and then click on <u>New Incognito window</u>. (Keyboard Shortcut: Control + shift + n) (<u>Figure 2.2</u>)

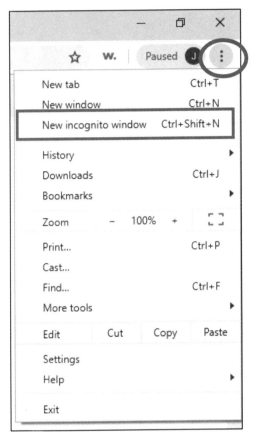

<u>Figure 2.2</u> – Google Chrome Web Browser -> Incognito Browsing

Safari: Click on <u>File</u> -> <u>New Private Window</u>. (Shortcut: command + shift + n) (<u>Figure 2.3</u>)

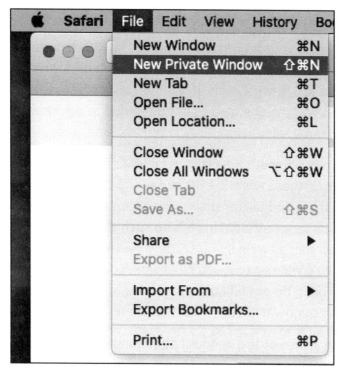

<u>Figure 2.3</u> – Safari (Apple) Web Browser -> Private Browsing

---

<u>Best Practice</u> – Most of the time, you will be just fine browsing the internet normally without private browsing. In fact, browsing the internet in private mode can make using some websites difficult. However, you should use private browsing whenever you do not want your activity and history to be collected and shared.

TIP: If you want to know exactly what type of information a certain website or browser is collecting and sharing, you can find out by visiting their privacy policy page. Most websites have a link to their privacy policy in the footer of their webpage. If the webpage does not have a privacy policy or it is extremely hard to find, use caution when browsing the website as they may be trying to hide their data collection practices.

Advertisements

Advertisements on the World Wide Web are everywhere, and they are not what they used to be. In the old days of the internet, advertisements were extremely inconvenient and would greatly interfere with the ability to browse the web. Remember annoying popups stating that you had won some prize? Fortunately, these types of ads are few and far between today, and most browsers will block annoying popups by default. Today's online advertisements are more neatly placed into convenient real estate and generally do not interfere with your ability to browse a website. Furthermore, ads today are tailored to align with your interests and online activity to better serve your needs. This is actually a good thing, as an advertisement in certain situations can help you find what you are looking for. Nevertheless, it is important for you to be able to recognize an advertisement when you see one, and to not be fooled by advertisements with malicious intent.

Let's start with the most obvious advertisement you should avoid, and that is the free lunch. Believe it or not, these ads still exist today and the reason they do is because people still click on them and fall for their scams. I am talking of course about the "Congratulations! You've won!" ad. **There is no such thing as a free lunch**, and this holds true on the internet as well. If you see an advertisement boasting about some prize, contest, or free giveaway that you have won, you should be wary about clicking on it. If you do click on it, do not fill out any forms that give away any of your personal information and do not download anything that it asks you to.

> **Best Practice** – Whenever you are in doubt about an advertisement, visualize whatever the advertisement is telling you in a real life situation, such as a random person on the street coming up to you and saying the exact thing to you that the advertisement is stating. This will help you put the ad in perspective and allow you to make a better choice on whether to indulge the ad.

Ad Blockers

Most desktop web browsers allow you to download extensions, which are software programs that add additional functionality to your browser. Ad blockers are one type of extension whose purpose is to prevent advertisements from appearing on your screen. These can be useful for you if you find yourself constantly inundated with pesky advertisements that are interfering with your ability to surf the web. On the other hand, the use of an ad blocker extension can make some websites completely unusable, and you will need to disable your ad blocker in order to view and interact with these websites.

Recommended Ad Blockers

- **CyberSec by NordVPN** – CyberSec is a security feature of NordVPN software which blocks ads and also protects you from malicious attacks on the internet, including certain types of malware. (www.nordvpn.com)
- **AdBlock** – AdBlock is a web browser extension that has a long history of successfully blocking ads in various mediums, including website ads, video ads, and some social media ads. (www.getadblock.com)

> **Best Practice** – Only use an ad blocker extension if you find yourself overwhelmed with advertisements that interfere with your ability to browse the web. This best practice does not apply if you use the Brave browser, which blocks all ads by default.

A Final Note on Ads

Advertisements play a very important role on the internet. They fund the majority of websites and allow for content creators to keep on creating, and ultimately lead to more innovation on the internet. Most ads that you will encounter are pretty straight forward, and as stated earlier, can actually help you in your browsing experience. Then there are the sneakier versions of advertisements that can be tricky to identify, and we will cover these next.

Referral Content

Referral content is any content that recommends or refers to some product or service in any way. There are two types of referral content out there on the World Wide Web, and they are *paid referral* and *free information*. Free information refers to content that may contain referrals to products or services where the author of the content does not have a financial interest in you using the products or services. Essentially, free information refers to content that is providing information to you with no ulterior motive. Conversely, paid referral content refers to content where the author has a financial interest in you using the recommended products or services.

Here is how paid referral content works. An author of an online article or blog writes about a product. Included in this article are links you can click on to buy the product. If you do click on a link and buy the product, the author of the content may receive a commission on the sale. This type of content is all over the internet, and it is not necessarily a bad thing. Many people who write blogs or run websites create referral links for products that they genuinely recommend, and hey, if you recommend something and people end up buying it why not take a little commission? The problem comes when articles recommend products *strictly* for the financial gain, and even worse, do not tell their readers that they receive a commission from any sale. In this type of case, the recommendation may be worthless to you.

Luckily, there are a few simple ways to check if a link in an article is a paid referral link. The first thing you can do is see if the author states anywhere that they receive a commission from their recommendations. If they do state this, then this is a positive sign that they are being honest about their recommendations. If you do not see any information from the author telling you that they collect commissions, a simple way to check if they might receive one is to hover your mouse over the link in the article, and then look at the web address (URL) the link would open if you click on it.

If the URL contains several unordered numbers and letters, then this may indicate that the link is a **paid referral**. On the other hand, if the URL looks standard and does not contain a long series of letters and numbers in no meaningful order, then this may indicate that the link is not a paid referral i.e. the author does not receive a commission if you buy the product. I use the term "may indicate" here because there really is unassailable way to tell, but the method I describe here should work for you the majority of the time.

Here is an example of free information content (Figure 2.4) and paid referral content (Figure 2.5).

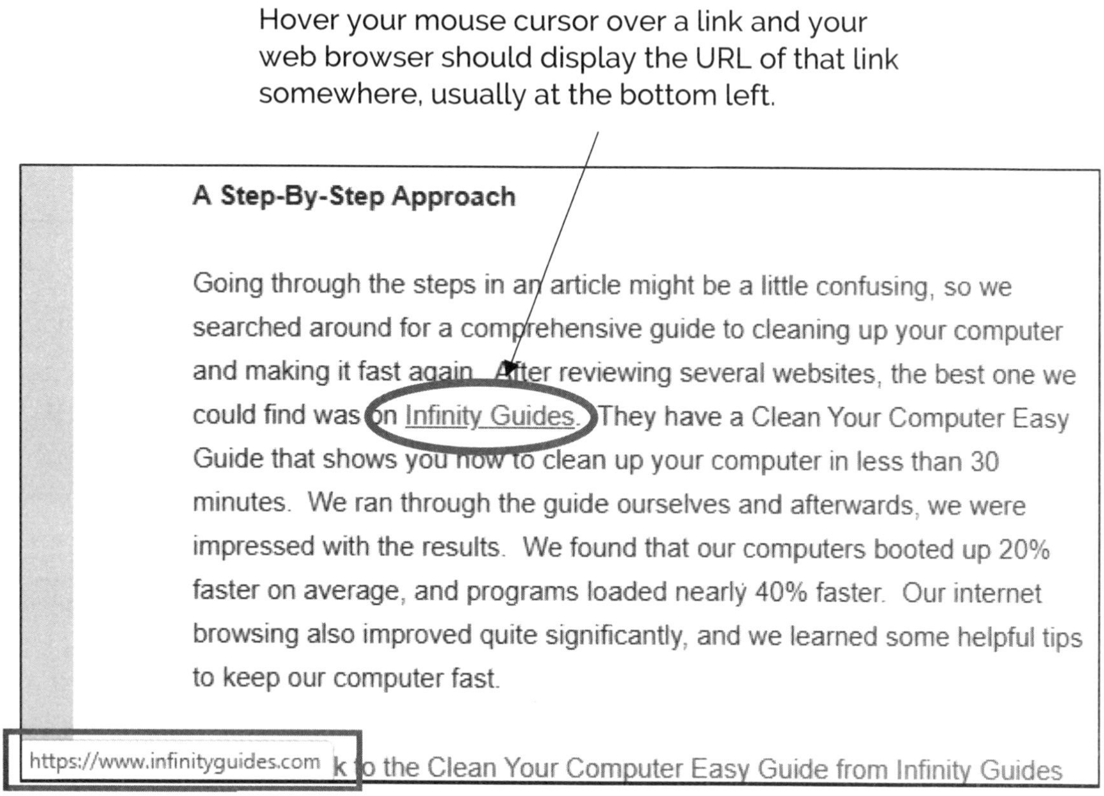

Hover your mouse cursor over a link and your web browser should display the URL of that link somewhere, usually at the bottom left.

A Step-By-Step Approach

Going through the steps in an article might be a little confusing, so we searched around for a comprehensive guide to cleaning up your computer and making it fast again. After reviewing several websites, the best one we could find was on Infinity Guides. They have a Clean Your Computer Easy Guide that shows you how to clean up your computer in less than 30 minutes. We ran through the guide ourselves and afterwards, we were impressed with the results. We found that our computers booted up 20% faster on average, and programs loaded nearly 40% faster. Our internet browsing also improved quite significantly, and we learned some helpful tips to keep our computer fast.

https://www.infinityguides.com k to the Clean Your Computer Easy Guide from Infinity Guides

Figure 2.4 – Free Information Content Example

Looking at Figure 2.4, it is clear that the link in the article goes directly to the website the author indicated since the URL matches the website name and the URL contains no obvious signs of referral codes.

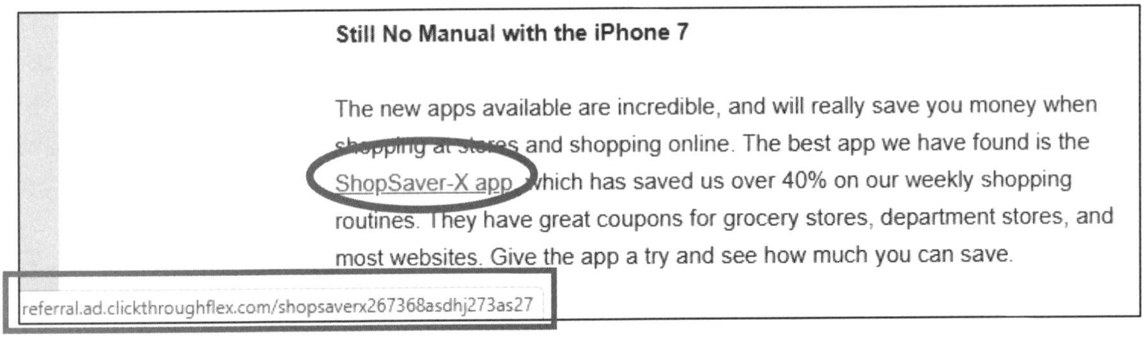

Still No Manual with the iPhone 7

The new apps available are incredible, and will really save you money when shopping at stores and shopping online. The best app we have found is the ShopSaver-X app, which has saved us over 40% on our weekly shopping routines. They have great coupons for grocery stores, department stores, and most websites. Give the app a try and see how much you can save.

referral.ad.clickthroughflex.com/shopsaverx267368asdhj273as27

Figure 2.5 – Paid Referral Content Example

Contrarily, looking at Figure 2.5, we can see that this link is very different than the link we examined in Figure 2.4. There are a few buzzwords in this link that *may* indicate that this recommendation is a paid referral, such as the words *ad* and *click*. Furthermore, the random series of letters and numbers in the link is another indication that this link *could* be a paid referral. There is no definite way to know for sure, but the clues for this link are all favoring the verdict that the link is indeed a paid referral.

Best Practice – If you ever suspect that an online recommendation is **only** being made to you for financial gain, and not for genuine purposes, hover your mouse over the link to see the URL, and look to see if it contains several unordered numbers and letters. If it does, your suspicions may be right and you should consider doing additional research. Remember, even if the link is a paid referral, it does not necessarily mean the content is disingenuous.

TIP: You can see more examples of free referrals and paid referral content online at www.infinityguides.com/blogs/news

Sponsored Content

If you have not heard of online sponsored content before, prepare to be a little surprised. Online sponsored content is defined as information that is written by an advertiser, but made to look like genuine content. Usually, you can find sponsored content structured as a news article on a news website, and its headline is often something that at first glance you would never think to be an advertisement. Before we explore this further, let me give you an example of sponsored content (Figure 2.6).

US Treasury Department Reports 70% Increase in Identity Theft

No Limit News thanks NLX Security for sponsoring this article.

The US Treasury Department reported on Monday a 70% increase in cases of identity theft reported by the Federal Bureau of Investigation. A spokesman for the FBI confirmed the report and stated at a press briefing that, "Identity thieves are increasingly stealing personal and financial information through intermediaries, such as credit bureaus and online marketplaces." The spokesman pledged that the FBI will be working with federal and state lawmakers to strengthen security regulations on companies that store financial data.

Cases of identity theft and identity fraud have been increasing year over year in the US for the past decade, and thieves have developed new tools to target consumers like never before. In the past, consumers would solely have to worry about their financial data being stolen while shopping at websites. That is no longer the case, says Jack Manulis of NLX Security, a financial data protection company based out of New York. "Thieves today are trying to hack the databases of big box retailers; which could potentially give them access to the credit cards of customers who shopped at the store. This makes everyone vulnerable."

We spoke with Mr. Manulis to discuss what consumers can do to make sure their financial data is protected, and what to do should they become a victim of identity theft. "The conventional wisdom is that consumers should actively monitor their credit card statements. Unfortunately, that doesn't help you if a thief goes on a spending spree with your credit cards and opens a loan in your name. The best defense today is to have Identify Theft Insurance, just like you would have car insurance." Identity theft insurance, commonly called ID Insurance, is insurance against identity theft. The way it works is the insurance provider actively monitors your credit report for you, and if an attack where to happen, you would be completely covered and the insurance provider would fight to secure your identity. You also would not be on the hook for any purchases the thief made with your stolen information up to a certain limit.

For more information on Identity Theft and ID Insurance, visit the NLX Security information site.

Figure 2.6 – Example of Sponsored Content

Let's examine this article. At first glance, one might assume that this article is a standard news piece stating that cases of identity theft have risen 70%. Our first clue that something is amiss here is the italicized subtitle: *No Limit News thanks NLX Security for sponsoring this article.* This subtitle right here, called a *disclosure*, gives away that this is actually a **sponsored article**, which means the intent of the article is to advertise something and not just report the news. In this particular example, the sponsored article is meant to advertise the company NLX Security and their Identity Theft Insurance. On most reputable news sites, any article that is sponsored by an advertiser in this way will generally have some type of disclosure such as the one shown in <u>Figure 2.6</u>. The disclosure can be written in several different ways, and is usually located either near the beginning of the article or at the end. Here are some other ways in which the disclosure may be written:

This article courtesy of Advertiser Name

This is a sponsored article by Advertiser Name. Advertiser Name can be visited by clicking <u>here</u>.

Our affiliate, Advertiser's name, contributed to this article.

This article presented in conjunction with our partners, Advertiser Name.

Determining if an article is sponsored content

Use these tips to help you determine if an article or blog post is sponsored content:

- First, look for a disclosure that indicates the article is sponsored content. Common keywords seen in such disclosures include: sponsored, affiliated, partners, contributed, etc. Disclosures can usually be found at the beginning or end of an article.
- Look for links in the article that direct you to purchase or sign up for some product or service. Links in news articles are common, especially when they are used as sources. Links in sponsored content however, are meant to direct you to the advertiser or to buy something.
- Look for the author's name at the beginning or end of an article. Most news sites and blogs sign their legitimate articles with the author's name, whereas sponsored content is sometimes signed by a company, link, or employee of the advertiser's company.

Determining if an article is sponsored content is beneficial because you want to know exactly what it is that you are reading. It is worthwhile to know if you are reading legitimate news or a pitch from an advertiser.

Fake News

You have probably heard the term fake news before, as it has been commonly discussed in the media over the past few years. Fake news does not necessarily pose a serious threat to you in any real way. Instead, if you fall victim to fake news you risk being misinformed or embarrassed, especially if you then go ahead and share that fake news. So in this section I will help you to recognize and identify fake news.

Fake news has plenty of definitions, but for the purpose of this book we will define fake news as a piece of information presented to be true that is inherently false. To understand why I even mention fake news in this book, we need to understand what its purpose is. Disregarding political purposes, the purpose of fake news is to get you to read it, become emotionally invested in it, and then share it. This will then lead to more people reading it and sharing it, which will lead to the creator of the fake news content making money. The more people that visit the website and read the fake news, the more money the creator makes from advertisements being shown to these readers. Hence, we have the financial motive for fake news.

How to Identify Fake News

If you suspect you are reading or viewing fake news, there are some steps you can take to determine if it's real.

- Check to see if the article contains sources with links, and check to make sure those links work. Many fake news creators will not bother citing sources with links in their articles, and will instead just make up their own sources.
- Check to see if the article has an author signed to it, and check to see if that author is real. Many fake news articles will not show an author's name because the real author does not want to be associated with false information. Furthermore, if the article does list an author, you can do a quick internet search for the author's name and see if this person exists and is in fact an arbiter of news.
- If the article does have a legitimate author, make sure that particular author actually wrote the article. You can usually check this by looking at the author's Facebook or Twitter profile and seeing if they made a post about the article.
- Check to see if another outlet is reporting the same news content as the suspected fake news article. You can check for this by performing a web search of the article's title and seeing if any other outlets are reporting the same story.

A word of caution: Unfortunately, fake news can be found on websites both big and small, so keep that in mind when reading articles from a so-called "trusted website".

In the grand scheme of things, fake news does not pose any real danger to you when you are browsing the web. The only risk you have is if you spread it and later you find out the news was fake, in which case you will have slightly embarrassed yourself.

Clickbait

Clickbait is a distasteful practice that is similar to fake news in many ways, and is widely prevalent throughout the internet. You can find clickbait all over social media, and it is a fairly popular advertising tactic as well. To define, clickbait is an article or post strictly meant to elicit an emotional response, which will in turn lead you to "click" on it. It's as simple as that. Let's examine the purpose of clickbait so you can better recognize it when you encounter it. Like fake news, the purpose of clickbait is to first get your attention with a headline that is meant to trigger a strong emotional response from you such as disbelief, outrage, awe, anger, hatred, etc. Then, the creator of the clickbait is hoping you will *click* on the headline or article to read more about it, and maybe even share it with other people. The more people that *click* on the clickbait, the more money the creator of the clickbait article makes from advertisements showing on their website.

The clickbait industry online is massive, and is used by nearly all content creators both big and small. It is especially prevalent in social media by both the creators of the clickbait content and by people who then share the clickbait for their own financial gain. Let me demonstrate this by giving you an example:

Example of Clickbait

1. No Limit News (NLN) creates an article headlined: *You Won't Believe What this High School Cheerleading Team was Caught Doing during Practice!*
2. NLN then shares the article and its headline on its website and on social media.
3. The article receives thousands of clicks, and NLN makes money from the advertisers that get to show their ads to all of the readers of the article.
4. Other people on social media notice that the article is gaining traction, so they begin sharing it and may even alter the headline and add commentary to get more people to click on it. These people are sometimes referred to as "influencers".
5. More people on social media see the clickbait and click on it because it was shared by influencers. Some of these people begin to "follow" and "like" the

influencers. A *follower* on social media is just someone who follows your account or profile.

6. The influencers' audiences grow larger, and they can then make money off of their larger audiences through advertisers and promotions.
7. NLN continues to gain more visitors to their website and make more money from advertisers.

See how this works? First, the website No Limit News (NLN) creates and posts the clickbait article to their website and social media in the hopes that people will see their intriguing headline and click on it. Once these people click on the headline, they are brought to NLN's website to read the article, and NLN makes money from their advertisers by showing their visitors ads. Furthermore, influencers on social media see the clickbait headline and realize they can push the article to gain attention and more followers; so they begin spreading the clickbait on their social media accounts and may even make the headline more intriguing. The influencers' followers see the clickbait headline and click on it, thus bringing more money to NLN when they visit their website. In turn, the influencers are getting more attention as other people on social media share the article, and it is likely that the influencers will gain more followers. The influencers may then later use the audience of followers that they have accumulated for their own financial gain. All the while the website that created the clickbait article and headline is raking in money as more and more people visit their website to read the article.

This example of clickbait is actually a business model for a large numbers of websites and influencers on the internet, and has proven to be very profitable for many of them.

> **Best Practice:** If you suspect an article may be clickbait, it probably is. Don't waste your time clicking on something that triggered a significant emotional response for the sake of getting your reaction. Ignore the headline and move on. Most clickbait articles have a misleading headline anyways and the content itself turns out to be underwhelming.

Sharing your Personal Information

You should always be skeptical whenever a website asks for information from you. You should never just give any of your information away online without expecting something in return, such as purchasing an item or signing up for a newsletter or service. Here are some general guidelines on what type of information you should and should not share online, and when it is appropriate to do so.

Your Email Address (Very safe, minimal risk)

Generally, sharing your email address online is a safe act that comes with minimal risk. The biggest risk of sharing your email address is it may lead to you receiving unwanted emails and spam if you share it at the wrong places. Once you have read the chapter on email safety, you will be well prepared to deal with these.

Your Phone Number (Safe, minimal risk)

I personally recommend you be a little more guarded with your phone number online than with your email address. An email address can easily be changed, and there are simple safeguards you can take to protect yourself from spam. On the other hand, your phone number is a little more personal, and you should use a little more caution when giving it out online.

Some websites may ask for your phone number for a variety of reasons, and here are some examples of when it is acceptable to do so:

- To purchase something online
- To use for two-step/factor verification
- To use as a password recovery tool
- To use as contact information (an example of this is if you are filling out a contact form on a website and prefer a phone call back)

In general, it is acceptable to share your phone number online when you are expecting your phone number to be used for something beneficial, such as the examples listed. The biggest risk of sharing your phone number online is that you may receive unwanted phone calls and text messages, particularly from telemarketers. I also recommend that you never publicly display your personal phone number on social media.

Your Name and Address (Situational risk)

You will almost always have to provide your name, billing address, and shipping address whenever you purchase something online. We will cover this in more detail in Chapter 3.

Your Financial Information

As with your name and address, you will be required to provide some financial information such as your credit card details when purchasing something online. We will cover this in more detail in Chapter 3.

Your Social Security/Driver's License/Tax ID/Passport Number or Similar (Very high risk)

You should rarely, if ever, provide your social security number to a website, unless that website is highly regulated by the government. Examples of when it may be okay to share this information is when you are applying for a bank loan or some other financial service, or when you are using a government website.

You can tell if you are using a government website by looking at the top level domain (TLD) of the web address (.com, .org, .gov, .net, etc.) Please note that not all countries have a TLD for their government websites, in which case you should use extreme caution when sharing your very sensitive information.

Here is the TLD's for various country's governments:

Country	Top Level Domain
United States	.gov
Canada	.gc.ca
Australia	.gov.au
United Kingdom	.gov.uk

For a full list of government TLDs, visit www.infinityguides.com/blogs/news

Best Practice: Always use caution whenever you are asked to divulge personal information on the internet. The less information you give out, the better. If you ever find yourself in doubt as to whether you should share information to a website, ask a trusted friend or better yet ask me: you can always write to me on Facebook (@JoeMalacina1 / www.facebook.com/joemalacina1) or Twitter (@JoeMalacina / www.twitter.com/joemalacina) and I will give you my best advice.

Chapter 3 – Online Shopping Safety

Shopping online can be a wonderful, expedient, and pleasant experience. There are millions of websites and apps that allow you to shop online from the comfort of your home, and you can literally shop online for anything you could nearly think of. With that said however, there are still some basic practices you must follow when shopping online to keep your financial information safe, and to keep yourself from getting scammed. In this chapter we will explore all of the best practices you should follow when shopping online.

The 1st Rule: SSL Security

The 1st Rule is ironically the least known rule of online shopping, and that is making sure that whatever website you are shopping at has an SSL certificate. SSL stands for Secure Sockets Layer (which you do not need to remember), and an SSL certificate secures your internet connection to the website so that any data transferred between you and the site, such as your credit card and login information, is secured. In other words, a SSL certificate prevents any of your data from being stolen while it is transmitted over the internet.

An SSL certificate is already the standard in online shopping safety and you should use the utmost caution when buying anything from any website that does not have one.

How to check if a Website has an SSL Certificate

Checking to see if a website has an SSL certificate is extremely easy: your web browser will do it for you. On most web browsers, your browser will show a padlock icon somewhere near the address bar at the top of your screen whenever you are on an SSL secured website. Some web browsers will also color the address bar green to indicate the website is secure. If the website does not have an SSL certificate, some web browsers will make a point to indicate this to you either with text stating "Not Secure" or a crossed out padlock. Figures 3.1 & 3.2 show various web browsers on websites with SSL certificates and those without.

Another way you can check if a website has an SSL certificate is to look at the URL of the website in the address bar. If the website has an SSL certificate, the beginning of the URL will start with https:// instead of http://.

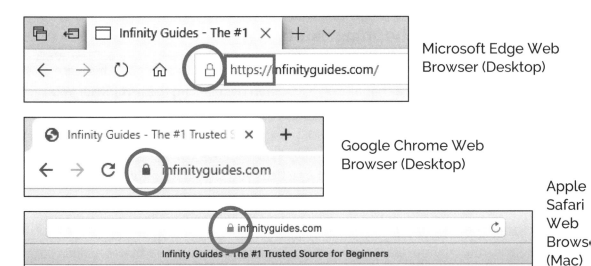

Figure 3.1 – Examples of SSL Secured Websites on Edge, Chrome, & Safari

Figure 3.2 – Examples Websites without SSL Certificate on Edge, Chrome, & Safari

Note: You only need to make sure that payment pages have SSL certificates, not the entire website. For instance, the home page of a website may not have an SSL certificate and that is OKAY. However, when the time comes for you to enter in your financial information, you should absolutely be sure that this particular page has an SSL certificate by looking at your address bar.

Note: It is completely normal and okay for a website that does not sell anything to NOT have an SSL certificate. An SSL certificate is only prudent when you need to enter sensitive personal or financial information, such as your credit card details.

> **Best Practice:** When shopping online, always do a quick check in your web browser to see if the website has an SSL certificate **while you are on the payment details page**. If the website does not have an SSL certificate (known as not secure), do not enter any payment details unless you are paying using a third-party payer such as PayPal, which should have SSL security itself.

Paying for Online Purchases

There are a few simple best practices you can follow when going to pay for online purchases that will put you in the best position to keep your financial information secure and protect yourself from fraud. The first thing to know is what type of information you may typically be asked for when shopping online.

Information that you will typically be asked for when shopping online

- Name
- Email address
- Billing address
- Shipping address
- Phone number
- Payment method
- Payment details
    - Credit card number
    - Credit card expiration date
    - Credit card billing postal code
    - Name as it appears on your credit card

Information that you should never provide when shopping for something online

- Your social security number or personal tax identification number

Some websites may ask for some additional information, and you can be the best judge as to whether that request is reasonable for the product or service you are purchasing.

The 2nd Rule: Never Use a Debit Card, Electronic Check, or Bank (ACH) Transfer to Pay Online

This is another rule that is unfortunately not widely known. When purchasing something online, never use a debit card, electronic check, or bank transfer as your method of payment. The reason being is simple: you want to limit your financial exposure as much as possible.

Let me give you an example of why you should follow this rule. Let's say you purchased something online from the company FunOnlineWidgetsNLX.com, and use a bank transfer (sometimes referred to as an ACH transfer) to provide your payment. The website you purchased from is secure and everything goes as planned and you receive your purchased goods. Then, six months later you find out that the FunOnlineWidgetsNLX.com Company was hacked by an outside group and their customers' financial data was breached. Whoever hacked the company may now have your bank account number and its routing number, because you had to provide these numbers in order to complete the ACH transfer. In other words, they potentially have direct access to your bank account and the funds associated with it. This is not a situation you want to be in, as your only remedy is to contact your bank and change your account number before any damage can be done. Changing your bank account number can be a real hassle and cause all sorts of problems for you. This type of situation can be easily prevented by **always using a credit card or third-party payer to purchase items online**.

Let's examine the same example again, only this time let's see what happens if you used a credit card instead. In this case, when the company gets hacked only your credit card details are available to the hackers. The hackers have no access to your bank account and no access to your actual money. Instead, the most damage they can do is limited to the credit limit of your credit card. This is still a troubling situation, but your exposure in this case is significantly less than the prior example. Now to remedy this situation all you would need to do is call your credit card company and get a new card with a new number. Moreover, if the thieves do end up using your credit card fraudulently, you can call your credit card company and let them know that you did not authorize those purchases, in which case they will take action to prevent those charges from being completed.

> **Best Practice:** When purchasing goods or services online, ALWAYS use a credit card or third-party payer to complete payment. NEVER use a debit card, electronic check, or ACH bank transfer.

Note: Some government websites may require you to pay with an electronic check or bank transfer, simply because there is no processing fee for doing so.

Third-Party Payers

A third-party payer is an intermediary you can use to make a payment for something on your behalf. They exist to provide additional security for you, and to provide you with more peace of mind when making an online purchase. Many of these payers also offer some sort of buyer protection, which can protect you from suffering the consequences of making a purchase at a fraudulent website. Here is how it works:

You would first need to sign up and create an account with a third-party payer, such as PayPal. To create an account with one of these, you will have to enter your personal and financial information. The financial information you may have to divulge includes your name, address, bank account information, and a credit card which will be used to make purchases. You also may have to provide your social security or tax number to verify your identity. Then when you go to make a purchase, many websites allow you to pay using a third-party payer, in which case you would login with your account and complete the payment.

To summarize, a third-party payer is an additional layer of protection between you, your financial details, and the website you are making a purchase from. When you use a third-party payer, the website you are buying from will never see your credit card or bank details, as they instead will charge the third-party directly, and the third-party payer will then charge your payment method and handle the transaction.

Here is a short list of my recommended third-party payers:

- **PayPal** – The most popular third-party payer, and it has a long history of security and reliability. Many sites also accept PayPal as a form of payment. You can sign up with them at www.paypal.com
- **Google Pay** – Newer than PayPal, Google Pay is another third-party payer with excellent security features. The only downside is they are not accepted at as many websites as PayPal is. You can sign up at https://pay.google.com.
- **Amazon Pay** – Allows you to use your Amazon account to make purchases. Also not as widely accepted as PayPal. You can sign up at www.amazon.com.

A third-party payer is a safe way to make purchases online, and I recommend you use one whenever you are making a purchase from a website you do not trust. Otherwise, always use a credit card to make an online purchase.

Best Practice: Use a third-party payer, such as PayPal, when purchasing something from a website that you do not trust enough to use your credit card. When paying using a third-party payer, make sure you are logging in to the correct website of the third-party payer (i.e. paypal.com).

Online Receipts

Just as like when you are shopping at a physical store, you should always make sure you get a receipt when you purchase something online. Receipts from websites are usually sent to your email address, so make sure you enter your email address in correctly when checking out from a website. Receipts can arrive anywhere between one minute and twenty-four hours after making a purchase, and you should keep your receipts in a folder on your email account.

Best Practice: Create a folder in your email account and name it "Receipts". Move all receipts you receive through email into this folder and keep them for at least six months.

Trusting Websites

If you follow the two rules outlined in this chapter, you are already well on your way to protecting yourself while shopping online. With that said, if you come across a website that you do not trust for some reason, there are some things you can look for to find out if it is trustworthy.

What to Look for in a Website when Shopping Online

- **Check for SSL Certificate** – See the 1st Rule
- **See if they offer payment by third-party payers** – If a website allows you to pay using a third-party provider, such as PayPal, Google Pay, or Amazon Pay, that is a great sign. This is not necessary for a website to be legitimate, but it certainly helps.
- **See if the website offers contact information** – Every website that allows you to purchase something should definitely have a contact page that allows you to easily contact them through email, online form, or phone. This contact page should be easy to find either in the navigation section of the website or in the

footer. Furthermore, if the website lists their email address, make sure their email address ends in the same domain as the website and does not have a popular domain ending instead. (Example: If you are shopping at www.infinityguides.com, if they list a contact email on their website make sure it ends in @infinityguides.com instead of something like infinityguides@aol.com.) Do not expect websites to list their phone number, as this is becoming less of a practice these days.

- **Check to see if the website has a privacy policy and a terms of service** – This is a standard practice of all major websites, and you can usually find these in the footer of the site. They will be listed as *Privacy Policy* and *Terms of Use*, *Terms of Service*, or *Terms and Conditions*.

- **Check to see if their copyright year is updated** – Nearly all websites have a copyright line in the footer of their website, and it usually states something along the lines of: "Copyright XXXX Company Name", where the XXXX is the current year and the Company Name is the name of the website or the name of the company that runs the website. Check the year in the copyright line and make sure it is up to date. Sometimes this year can be off by one, especially if it is January or February and they have not gotten around to updating it, and this is usually no big deal. However, if you come across a website whose copyright year is off by two years or more, then you should use extra caution if you decide to purchase something from that site. The reason being is a copyright statement that has not been updated in two or more years could indicate a webmaster who is either lazy or incompetent; and any website that is that incompetent with a simple copyright title may also be incompetent when it comes to keeping up with today's standards in website security.

- **If you are still in doubt, check to see where the company/website is headquartered** – What you really want to find out here is if the company or person that owns the website is located in a country that you are comfortable purchasing from. You can find this out in a couple different ways. The quickest way to find this out is to look in the footer and in the *Terms of Use*. Sometimes in the footer you can find the country the company is located in. If it is not listed, look at the *Terms of Use* and look for a line that states "Subject to the laws of…" At the end of this sentence should be the state/province and country of the company. This is normally located in the first paragraph. If you cannot find anything on where the company is headquartered, then you may be dealing with a foreign website posing as a domestic one. You can also perform a web search of the website's name to see if you can come up with any information.

Online Shopping Tips

To close out this chapter, I will leave you with a few tips to help you have a safe and happy experience shopping online.

1. Follow the 1st and 2nd rules of shopping online. Always make sure the website you are buying from is SSL secured and never pay using an electronic check or ACH bank transfer. A credit card or third-party payer is the preferred method of payment for best security. If you do not have a credit card, then a debit card is far more preferable than an electronic check or bank transfer.
2. When completing the checkout process of a website, make sure you enter your details accurately, including your email address and shipping details. Failure to provide this data accurately could result in problems later on.
3. Avoid shopping on websites that are based in countries that have a history of ripping off consumers. There are many websites out there that appear to be based in the U.S. or Europe that are in fact based in third world or developing countries, and you should avoid purchasing anything from these websites. Unfortunately, the security standards in place on these websites are often lax compared to western nations, and you will have little recourse in getting your money back if something were to go wrong. If you think you have encountered a website like this, you can check by looking at the Terms of Use to see if they have a "Subject to the laws of..." statement. Another clue to look for is if their shipping and delivery time is unusually long (such as if delivery is estimated to take a month).
4. Always make sure you get an email receipt for anything you purchase online. Keep your receipts and save them in a *Receipts* folder in your email account.

Chapter 4 – Email Safety

Email is a wonderful tool that has found its way into nearly every household and office in the United States. According to data from Statista, over 269 billion emails were sent and received *each day* in 2017, and that number is expected to grow each and every year. With so many emails being sent and received daily, you will no doubt come across an email that attempts to scam you in some way. In this chapter, I will show you how to use email safely online by following my tried and true best practices. Furthermore, I will teach you how to identify a scam, and what to do when you encounter one.

Built-In Safety

Before we begin covering everything you need to know about email safety, it is important to recognize that you already have some built-in protection against many of the worst email attacks. The first layer of protection is your email account provider. A provider is basically the host of your email, and some common providers include Gmail, AOL, Hotmail, Comcast, and ATT. Many of these providers have built in spam and malicious email filtering that will prevent you from receiving some emails with malicious intent. Sometimes, emails with viruses or hijacking software attached will be stopped cold from ever reaching your inbox by your provider. This is important to know so you can make better decisions about who you choose to use as an email provider. If you decide you want to create a new email address in the future, my advice would be to pick a well-known provider that has a substantial amount of users. That way, you can have confidence that your provider has the tools and experience to protect you from some of the most dangerous email attacks.

If your computer or device has antivirus software, then you also have another layer of built-in protection. Most antivirus software applications scan your emails for any harmful attachments, and will notify you when it comes across one. Antivirus protection can be an excellent tool to keep your device, especially your computer, safe.

Spam & Junk Mail

The first type of fraudulent email that you have most likely heard about and are bound to come across is spam. Spam mail, sometimes known as junk mail, is defined as unwanted email that solicits you in some way. Spam mail can appear in many shapes and sizes, and can be pretty harmful to boot. Luckily, most email accounts and email software programs have excellent spam filters that catch this junk and move it immediately to your spam or junk folder. With that said, your spam filter is not perfect, and some spam is bound to get through and you will have to deal with it.

Recognizing a Spam Email

Most spam email messages are easily recognizable. The telltale signs are many links in the message, too good to be true news or solicitation, no unsubscribe option, and the email is from a sender you have never heard about. Other, non-threatening types of spam can be legitimate emails with news or information that you just do not want to read. Either way, spam is a nuisance and there are steps you can take to reduce the amount of spam and junk mail you receive and protect yourself from falling prey to its promises.

See Figures 4.1 and 4.2 to see examples of what spam mail can look like.

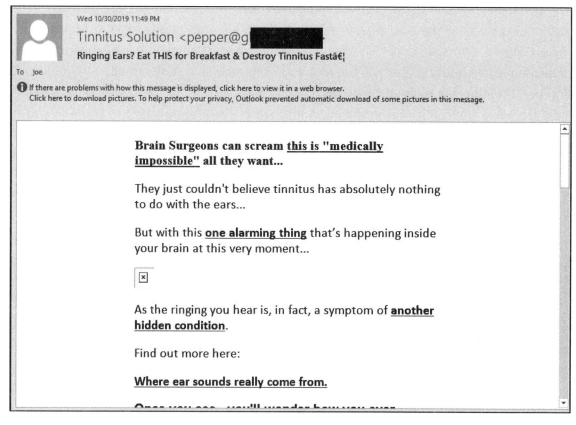

Figure 4.1 – Example of a Spam or Junk Email

Let's examine Figure 4.1 and see how this email is obviously spam and how it should immediately be reported and moved to my junk folder. The first glaring clue is the subject of the email and the identity of the sender. First and foremost, I do not have tinnitus and have no memory of ever having visited any websites that have anything to do with tinnitus, so why in the world am I receiving this email? Secondly, I have never heard of the company that is sending me this email and their web address is also unknown to me. From these two indications alone I can label this email as spam. If I want to investigate further, I can take one look at the body of the email and easily see that it is riddled with indicators of spam. The most glaring example is the obscene amount of links in the body. This email is begging me to click on any of these links (which are all underlined) and this desperation is a telltale sign of spam. Moreover, the poor grammar used in the message body also indicates that this email is clearly spam. Now let's examine a more subtle example (Figure 4.2):

Figure 4.2 – Example of a Spam or Junk Email

This email looks nothing like the spam mail we examined in <u>Figure 4.1</u>. Nevertheless, through a mild investigation we can determine that the email is indeed spam. The first thing to look at is the sender, which is someone I do not recognize nor recall ever conversing with. The second thing to look at is the sender's email address, which points to a website I do not recall ever visiting. Thirdly, the subject of the email is suspicious, as it indicates that the message is a reply because of the "Re:" portion. Well if this email truly was a reply then I would be able to see the original email I sent to him at the bottom of this email message, which of course is not present. So far this email has many indicators that would lead me to treat it as suspicious, so let's move on to the body of the email.

In the body of the email you may have noticed that the sender addressed me using my real name. You may think that this is a positive indicator, but in fact, it is not. It is very easy for senders of spam to find out your first and last name, and just because your name is in the body of the email does not mean the message is legitimate. The last thing that is suspicious is the disclosure of his message, which at the end states, *"If you do not want further emails from me, please send any reply."* This line right here is the 100% proof that this email is spam and was unsolicited. No person who you regularly exchange emails with would put this in their disclosure, and the notion that you can send any reply to stop the emails from coming to you is absurd. If you received any email like this from an unknown sender, then you should NOT reply and instead report the message as spam or junk and delete it.

What to Do When you Encounter Spam

First of all, any spam that is sent to your Spam or Junk folder that you do not want, just leave it there or delete it. As long as it remains in your spam folder it cannot harm you so long as you do not read it or click on anything inside the message. Occasionally, some spam will make it past your spam filter and you will have to deal with it. Here is what you should do:

1. When you first encounter an email that you suspect is spam, first decide what type of email it is. Is it from a website you have genuinely used before? Is it from a newsletter you have subscribed to? Or is it **true spam**, which is from a sender you have never heard of and never want to hear from again? We will learn how to deal with the first two types later, but if you encounter **true spam**, then proceed to step 2.

2. The first and most important thing you can do when you encounter true spam is **flag the message as spam/junk**. This will alert your email provider that the message you received is spam, and they will report it as spam to their security system. In turn, their security system has a better chance of stopping similar spam emails from ever reaching your inbox in the future. When logged into your email account on your provider's website, there is usually an option somewhere to flag a message as spam or move it to junk.

3. After you have flagged a message as spam, **delete the message** if your provider has not already automatically deleted it or moved it to your junk folder.

4. If you encounter the same type of spam again, flag it again, and then delete the message.

5. If the same type of spam continues to plague your inbox, then your email address might actually be subscribed to the sender, in which case you can try to unsubscribe yourself from the sender by looking for an unsubscribe link in the email message. Otherwise, keep flagging the messages as spam and deleting them.

   a. **Important:** If you try to unsubscribe yourself from a sender that is clearly true spam, NEVER enter any of your information, including your email address, into the unsubscribe page that opens up. The sender may just be trying to figure out if you are a real person, and once you enter your email address into their phony unsubscribe page, then they know you are real and will probably double up on the spam and share your email address with more spammers.

Newsletters and Previously Used Websites

It is completely normal to receive emails from websites that you have used in the past and have given your email address to. These emails are usually purposed to deliver you specific information about actions you have taken on their website, such as providing you with a receipt or tracking information for an order. You should not flag these messages as spam, as that may prevent you from receiving emails from them in the future. Instead, you should try to **unsubscribe** from these emails only if they have become bothersome. To unsubscribe from unwanted emails from a genuine sender, follow these steps:

1. Look in the email for a link to unsubscribe (Figure 4.3). Click on the link to unsubscribe.

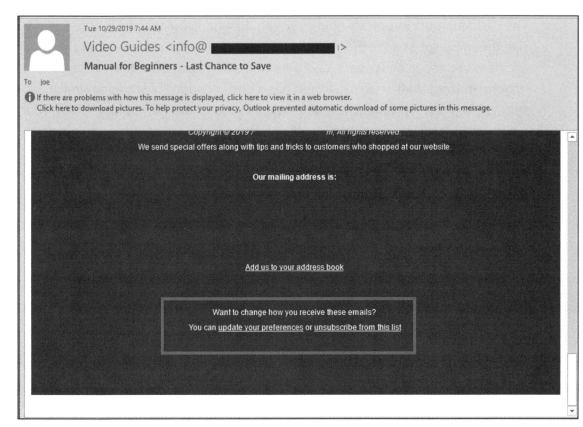

Figure 4.3 – Unsubscribing from an Email List

2. A webpage should open, and hopefully the page will tell you that your email address has been unsubscribed from their lists. You may have to choose which type of emails you no longer want to receive from the sender. Go ahead and do so.

3. Some websites may ask you to enter your email address so that they can properly unsubscribe it from their mailing lists. Be wary when you encounter this. If you recognize the site and trust them, you can probably go ahead and follow their instructions. If you are unsure, then do not take the chance and do not enter your email address.

4. Once you have unsubscribed you should stop receiving emails from the sender within 72 hours. If emails keep recurring, try unsubscribing again. If that fails, treat the message as true spam and flag it.

Newsletters, on the other hand, are emails that you receive from a website or person that you have subscribed to. Email newsletters can be incredibly helpful, and should not be treated as spam unless you have never heard of the sender before. I am subscribed to 8 newsletters myself, mostly about technology, health, and fitness, and I find them very beneficial to my work and life. I also have an email newsletter that I write each week, and I send it out to my over 50,000 subscribers. If you would like to subscribe to my newsletter, you can do so by visiting my website www.joemalacina.com.

On the flip side, if you are tired of receiving a specific newsletter, you can easily unsubscribe from one by following the same steps we just covered.

Phishing Emails

Now we get to some of the serious stuff when it comes to fraudulent emails, and we start with phishing attacks. Phishing is derived from the word fishing, and it works by scammers casting out some bait (the email message), and seeing what they can catch. The sender is fishing for your information, and they will take whatever you give them and use them in whatever way they can for personal gain. Let's start by examining a real-life example of a phishing attack. This attack reportedly happened to a man in the United States in 2016, and resulted in the man unwillingly exposing his email password to an attacker. The attacker then used his password to download and access all of his personal emails.

Figure 4.4 reportedly is the phishing email that was used to hack the man's emails. Let's examine this email and see what we can learn from it, as phishing emails like this are extremely common.

```
>  *From:* Google <no-reply@accounts.googlemail.com>
>  *Date:* March 19, 2016 at 4:34:30 AM EDT
>  *To:*  ███████████ ⟩gmail.com
>  *Subject:* *Someone has your password*  ◄──────────────
>
>  Someone has your password
>  Hi Jack  ◄────────────────────
>
>  Someone just used your password to try to sign in to your Google Account
>  ██████████@gmail.com.
>
>  Details:
>  Saturday, 19 March, 8:34:30 UTC
>  IP Address: 134.249.139.239
>  Location: Ukraine
>
>  Google stopped this sign-in attempt. You should change your password
>  immediately.
>
>  CHANGE PASSWORD <https://bit.ly/1PibSU0>  ◄──────────────
>
>  Best,
>  The Gmail Team
>  You received this mandatory email service announcement to update you about
>  important changes to your Google product or account.
```

Figure 4.4 – Example of a Phishing Email

At first glance this email may appear completely legitimate, as many phishing emails appear to be. Any reasonable person might think to themselves that they need to listen to what this email is telling them and change their password. However, through closer inspection we can find some obvious and not-so-obvious signs that something is definitely fishy (pun intended) with this email. Arrows have been added to the email in <u>Figure 4.4</u> to all instances that appear suspicious.

The first questionable part of this email is the subject: "*Someone has your password*". That is an awfully strange subject to be coming from a company like Google, which tends to send automated emails with strict professionalism. The subject here sounds like it is trying to create an emotional response. Go ahead and say it out loud, "Someone has your password." Now if someone said that to you in your house you would rightfully panic, and that's the point. Phishing emails, like some spam, try to trigger your emotions to get you to stop thinking clearly. Then, while your judgment is clouded by your emotions, you are more likely to make an error in judgment, and that is exactly what the phisher wants. So that is the first fishy part of the email: the strange subject line from supposedly Google. A more appropriate subject line you would receive from Google for something like this is: "Suspicious Activity has been detected on your Account" or "Please Review your Security Preferences on Google". Nevertheless, the subject could be legitimate, so let's look at the email a little closer to see what else we might notice.

Well we do not have to look far to see our next clue. The very first line states "Hi Jack". Do you see any issues here? Well the very first thing I noticed is the lack of a comma after the word Jack. Sloppy grammar is another telltale sign that an email such as this may have malicious intent. It is even more significant that this email is supposedly from Google, a multi-billion dollar company, and apparently they do not know how to use a comma or a colon in a greeting. Yet grammar mistakes can happen, even for automated emails that have probably been sent over a thousand times by large companies such as Google, so this email may still be believable yet.

The rest of the email looks pretty legitimate. In fact, most of the body of the email looks like a legitimate security alert that you might receive from a big company, until we get to where it says <u>CHANGE PASSWORD</u>. The way the words CHANGE PASSWORD is written in all capitalized letters reminds me of the same concerns I had about the subject line. It seems silly that a company like Google would have CHANGE PASSWORD completely capitalized instead of in a nice bordered button or something similar. Furthermore, I think in this instance that the sender made the words all capitalized to trigger an emotional response from the reader, just like with the subject. In general, all capitalized letters signifies urgency and exclamation, and it is meant to capture your attention.

So far through examining this email we have discovered some inconsistencies that make this message slightly suspicious, but these inconsistencies do not truly tell us that we are in fact dealing with a fraudulent email. We need hard evidence that this email is not what it says it is, and we can find that hard evidence by following this best practice.

> **Best Practice:** Always check links in suspicious or urgent emails that are urging you to disclose sensitive information such as your password. Be sure the links are directing you to the correct website with the correct domain.

So let's use this best practice when examining this email again. The link we are talking about in this email is the underlined text: CHANGE PASSWORD. We need to see where this link is going to bring us. Instead of clicking on the link to find out, we can hover our mouse over the link and see the URL. If you are viewing on a mobile device, you can generally tap and hold on a link to see its URL. In this case, we notice the URL is <https://bit.ly.1PibSU0> (Figure 4.4). This is EXTREMELY suspicious and it immediately tell us that this email is fraudulent. First off, any link in this email to change our password should point us to a Google site with a Google domain name (google.com). Secondly, a bit.ly link is known as a short link. A short link takes a long URL and shortens it to just a few characters. It is commonly used on social media, texting apps, and email to make links fit nicely into posts, however it should not be used in a security alert email, especially one asking you to change your password. This evidence alone makes it clear that this email is fraudulent, and it should be reported as spam and deleted immediately.

Let us take what we have learned from this example and derive some rules and best practices to follow when dealing with emails to keep you safe.

Checking Links in Email Messages

In this section I will show you how to properly check a link in an email message. This section is also relevant for any other links you may come across on the internet, whether they be on social media or on another website.

Links are a common practice in emails and the internet in general. Most of the links you will encounter are completely legitimate and pose no threat to you or your safety, and you should be able to use them freely. However, whenever you come across an email that is **suspicious** in some way, you should check the link to make sure it is bringing you to the right place. *You can check a link by either hovering your mouse over the link, or by clicking on the link to open it and checking your address bar at the top.*

The first thing you want to look for when examining a URL or link is to see if the domain is correct. A URL's domain is the last piece of text that comes before the last .com, .org, .net, etc. and after any periods preceding it.

Here are some examples:

URL (Web Address)	Domain
http://myaccount.nolimitcorp.com/loginresource12231	nolimitcorp.com
https://www.infinityguides.com	infinityguides.com
https://myaccount.nolimitcorp.com-securityx43.tk/signin122	com-securityx43.tk
http://reset.infinityguides.com-accountsettings44.rn/acnt	com-accountsettings44.rn

Let's look at the first URL, http://myaccount.nolimitcorp.com/loginresource12231. When trying to decipher what the domain is, you want to look for the **last piece of text before the <u>last period</u> and before the first slash after http:// or https://**. This may look and sound confusing, but understanding which domain a link is directing you to in a suspicious email is crucial for your security. So in the first link, the domain is nolimitcorp.com. It is not myaccount, as there is another period after it and before the backslash. The full domain is myaccount.nolimitcorp.com, where myaccount is the subdomain and nolimitcorp.com is the primary domain. All that we need to bother ourselves with is the primary domain which is nolimitcorp.com. So for this link we know that the domain is nolimitcorp.com, which means the link is part of the main website, www.nolimitcorp.com. Nolimitcorp.com is a safe and standard website, so any link that has that domain is safe to use.

Let's now look at the second URL. This is a pretty standard link that would bring us to the homepage of www.infinityguides.com, and infinityguides.com is the domain. This is a completely safe website to use.

Now let's look at the third URL. What do you think the domain is for this URL? If your answer is nolimitcorp.com, then you would be wrong. This URL is designed to make you think nolimitcorp.com is the domain, when in fact the domain is com-securityx43.tk. Remember, the domain is the last piece of text before the backslash, after any previous periods, and before the final .com, .org, .net, .etc. This URL is clearly fraudulent, as it is meant to make you think you are actually visiting a page on nolimitcorp.com when in fact you are not. What's worse is the creator of a fraudulent URL like this will design their website to look just like the site they are trying to imitate.

Finally, let's look at the fourth URL. What do you think the domain is in this one? The correct answer would be com-accountsettings44.rn. Again, this URL is clearly fraudulent and possibly dangerous and is designed to make you think you are visiting a page of infinityguides.com.

Best Practice: Always examine a link or URL in a **suspicious** email. Make sure the URL of the link is directing you to the proper domain, and beware of URLs that are designed to fool you.

Email Attachments

Sending and receiving attachments through email is a common practice, and is a great way to quickly send files to another person. Some caution should be exercised when you receive an attachment inside an email. Attachments in emails are how hackers can infect your computer or device with viruses and malware, and once your device is infected with malicious software, it can be extremely difficult to remove it and make your device safe again. Luckily, there are some rules and best practices you can follow to make sure you protect yourself from malicious attachments.

Best Practice #1: Do not open attachments from any email you consider suspicious. If in doubt, only open attachments from senders you are *expecting* to receive an attachment from.

This should go without saying, but you should NEVER open an attachment from a sender you are not familiar with or have never heard of. You also should take caution when you receive an unwarranted attachment from someone you do know. As you will see later, you cannot always trust the "from" email address that appears in an email message. That is why the *expecting* portion of the best practice is so important.

Best Practice #2: Never, under any circumstances, open an attachment that has a file extension of .exe, .iso, or .bat.

These type of files can make changes to your device or install malicious software. You should never open these type of files that are sent to you as an attachment, ever.

> **Best Practice #3:** If you do open an attachment that is suspicious, examine any links inside the attachment for domain accuracy. Be wary of any attachment files that direct you to click on a link.

This is a common practice of scammers. They will send you an attached file that looks innocuous, such as a Word document or PDF, but inside the document will be a link that they urge you to click on. You should absolutely be suspicious of any unsolicited attachments that you open and that direct you to click on a link. For some reason, scammers think an attachment makes an email look more legitimate, and that people will be more likely to click on a link that is inside an attachment. Fortunately for you, you have this book and will not be making that mistake.

Common Fraudulent Emails

Although new ways of scamming people through email are seen each and every day, the methods scammers use to defraud their victims have followed many of the same themes over the past 20 years.

Common Spam – Soliciting Emails

These types of emails are solicitous in nature and received against your will. The two main risks of falling for this type of scam are purchasing nonexistent or fraudulent merchandise and theft of credit card information. These emails commonly follow these themes:

- Promoting sexual vitality products
- Promoting online sexual or pornographic services
- Selling miracle cures to serious conditions and diseases
- Offering free money and prizes
- Offering to trade merchandise
- Unknown people soliciting your financial assistance
- Unknown people offering a reward for your assistance

The last bullet point is a very common scam that many people fall victim to and has serious consequences. Here is generally how it happens: a person will email you and tell you a story; their story is that they are from a foreign country and need help accessing some money that is locked away in an account. Sometimes they go as far as to tell you that they are a prince or someone of royalty. Then they say that all you need to do is wire them a relatively small amount of cash, say $500, and in return they will give you a percentage of the large amount of cash that they need help accessing. That percentage usually amounts to a very generous sum, say $50,000, and that is the lure of the trap. Do not fall for this scam and remember there is no such thing as a free lunch. To better protect yourself from scams like these, follow this next best practice.

> **Best Practice:** If you receive an email that is too good to be true, it probably is. Always treat a suspicious email as if a stranger on the street came up to you and said the exact content of the email to your face. That will help you put it in perspective.

Common Phishing Emails

Phishing emails are meant to trick you into giving up your sensitive information, such as account passwords and credit card details. These emails can be very sly and designed to look very real. These emails commonly follow these themes and often focus on these types of content:

- Your account has been hacked, please change your password
- Please reset your password
- Suspicious activity has been detected on your account
- Your credit card information is at risk
- Please agree to our new terms and conditions
- Action Required: Please login to your account

These common examples demonstrate why phishing attacks can be so hard to recognize, as the examples above are often legitimate and real. Follow these best practices to help you distinguish between a real email and a phishing email, and to protect yourself from becoming a victim of a phishing attack.

> **Best Practice:** When you come across an email that is directing you to change your password or login to your account, examine the links in the email for the proper domain.

This was covered extensively earlier in this chapter, and is extremely important for protecting yourself from a phishing attack. If checking links for proper domains is not your thing or you find it too hard to understand, there are other best practices you can follow that will accomplish the same thing.

> **Best Practice:** Consider any email that directs you to reset your password or login to your account as suspicious, **if you were not expecting to receive that email.**

This is a very important best practice. Any email you receive that is instructing you to reset your password or login to your account should immediately be treated as suspicious if you were not expecting to receive that email. When you are expecting that email, then you can treat that email as legitimate and safe. An example of when you can expect an email like this is if you forget your password to a website, and you click on the *Forgot Password* link. Usually, the website will send you an email immediately after you have clicked on this link and entered your email address so that you can reset or recover your password. They will also tell you that they are sending you an email, so therefore you can expect to receive and treat it as safe and legitimate.

Again, treat any email that directs you to reset your password or login to your account as suspicious if you were not expecting to receive that email.

> **Best Practice:** If you receive a *suspicious* email that directs you to reset your password or login to your account, go to the supposed website **manually** instead of clicking on any links within the email.

Let's demonstrate this with a quick example. Let's say you receive an email completely out of the blue from Yahoo directing you to change your password as they have detected suspicious activity. This email might be legitimate, but you were not expecting it and therefore you treat it as *suspicious*. At the same time you are now worried that your account is at risk and you want to take action. So what should you do?

The best practice dictates that you should not click on any links inside the email, and instead open up your web browser and go to www.yahoo.com and login. This is called going to a website manually rather than going through a link. This way, you are protecting yourself from potentially falling for a phishing scam by logging in directly to a website you know and trust. Now when you log in to Yahoo, if there really was a security threat, Yahoo might tell you the moment you log on. Or if you want to take extra precaution, you can go ahead and actually change your password on Yahoo and it would be completely safe to do so since you accessed their website manually instead of through an email link.

Common Attachment Scams

The last type of common fraudulent emails you are bound to come across are attachment scams. Email attachments can be particularly dangerous, so extra caution should be exercised when you come across a suspicious email with an attachment. Here are some examples of common attachment scams that contain these types of content:

- Invoice from a company (usually a PDF attachment)
- Please review this payment (usually a PDF)
- Your approval needed
- Help paying Invoice
- Check out this document! (usually a Word document or PDF)

The whole point of an attachment scam is to get you to open an attachment, and then possibly do something with the attachment. That being said, you should always use caution when you receive an email with an attachment. Never open an attachment from a sender that you do not recognize, and never click on a link inside an attachment from a completely unknown sender.

Best Practice: Never open an attachment in an email message from an unknown sender, and if you do open it, then do not click on any links inside the attachment. Never, under any circumstances, open an attachment that has the file extension types .exe, .iso, and .bat.

Never Trust a Name

If you recall the phishing email example we covered earlier in this chapter, I mentioned that you should never trust the name of the sender that appears in an email address. If you look back at Figure 4.4, we examined a phishing email from a sender posing to be Google. If you look at the header of that email message, you will notice that the sender was able to make his email address appear as a Google email address. Hence comes our next best practice:

Best Practice: If you come across a suspicious email, never use the *from email name* and *email address* as a way to authenticate the email's legitimacy.

The fact is, it is extremely easy for anyone to send an email and fake their name. It is as simple as changing your name in your email preferences. Moreover, more talented hackers can easily change the email address that appears in a message they send out. They can change it to show any email address they want, including your own. Therefore, you should never consider the email sender's email address when trying to determine if the email is fraudulent. (See Figure 4.4 as a reminder)

More Email Best Practices

There are a few additional best practices you can follow when using email to have a safe online experience. Some of these best practices do not specifically relate to safety, but are nonetheless helpful.

Best Practice 1: Email Naming Convention and Multiple Email Addresses

It is my recommendation that everyone should have at least two email addresses. One email address should be your personal email address, and should contain your first name and part or all of your last name. You would use this email address for all of your personal business and communication with friends and family. The naming convention for this personal email address is standard in today's online world as goes like this:

My name is Joe Malacina, therefore the personal email address I would create for myself would be something like:

- joemalacina@yahoo.com
- joe.malacina@yahoo.com
- joemal1@yahoo.com
- malacina.joe@yahoo.com

You would only use this email for personal communications with friends and family, and to conduct your personal business. Some people do not feel comfortable using any part of their real name in their email address, and that is okay if you fall into this category. In this case, you can set your personal email address to whichever you want, although I recommend you keep it short and have no more than four numbers.

The second email address you should create is known as your online identity. This email address should NOT contain any personally identifiable information, such as your first or last name. Instead, you should consider using a nickname or hobby for this email address. Examples of this are:

- baseballfan161@yahoo.com
- therealmanulis@yahoo.com
- cowboyusa1234@yahoo.com
- dontreadonme1776@yahoo.com

This is the email address you will be using to sign up for newsletters and social media, make online purchases, and share with potential internet strangers. You do not want any personally identifiable information in this email address as this is the one you are going to be making public to the internet, and it will no doubt see more spam than your personal email. Having two email addresses will help you recognize fraudulent emails more easily than if you were to only have one.

When creating any email address, stick with letters, numbers, and periods only. Do not use dashes, underscores, or symbols, and do not use more than four numbers. In addition, do not spread the numbers apart within your email address; keep them grouped together and never use the number 1 next to the letter L or I, as it can be extremely hard to differentiate between the two. Furthermore, capital letters mean nothing when creating an email address, as everyone will see your email address in all lowercases by default when you send them an email message.

Best Practice 2: Do NOT use your Internet Service Provider for your Email Address

Unfortunately, this best practice is not well known and it definitely needs to be. You do not want to use your internet service prover (ISP) as your main email provider. Examples of ISPs are Comcast, ATT, Windstream, Shaw, or whichever company supplies you with internet. When you sign up for internet service at your home, your ISP will pressure you to create an email address with them. You can do so if you would like, but I highly recommend that you never use that email address and create another one with an independent email provider instead. This is because your ISP email address is temporary. The moment you change who provides your internet or drastically change your plan, you could lose your email address and all of the messages and contacts you had with it.

Instead, create an email address with an independent provider that has a **.com, .net,** or **whatever your local top-level domain is (.com.au, .ca, etc.)** address. That way, you will have access to your email forever, no matter what happens to your ISP at home. There are hundreds of good email providers to choose from. Here are a couple of my recommendations:

- Outlook.com
- Gmail.com
- Yahoo.com
- Aol.com
- Reagan.com (Really great for privacy)
- Mail.com

- Protonmail.com (Great for privacy)
- iCloud.com (Apple)

It is important to note that many email providers scan your email messages in order to deliver you customized advertisements. This is a standard practice among providers and they claim that the information they scan remains encrypted so nobody on their side can read the actual content of your emails. Regardless, if this sort of thing really bothers you, then I recommend you check out either Reagan.com or Protonmail.com, who both claim that they do not track any of your email activity.

Chapter 5 – Social Media Safety

Social media has exploded in popularity to become a mainstream aspect of the internet on computers, smartphones, and other "smart" devices. There are several platforms that dominate the social media scene, and although each of these platforms are fun to use, they each come with their own specific risks and threats. In this chapter we will cover several of the most prominent social media platforms, and teach you how to be safe on each one. I will also show you the different types of threats you can expect to receive on the various platforms, and what you can do to protect yourself from these. Moreover, this chapter is especially helpful for parents, as children are some of the biggest users of social media and are often the most targeted by scammers and predators. So if you are a parent with dependent children, this chapter will educate you on how these social media platforms work. For specific risks to children using these platforms and what you can do to protect them, see Chapter 9.

The #1 Rule of Social Media

Every aspect of safety when using social media can be funneled down into one single rule which if recognized and understood, will lead you to make smart decisions when using any social media platform. That single rule is this one statement: **There is no such thing as privacy when using social media, and anything you share on social media will <u>forever</u> will be public**.

This is one powerful statement, and it is 100% true. The old saying goes, "The internet never forgets", and it rings more true today than ever before. Let's break down the different ways this rule applies to social media.

You cannot truly Delete Anything you Share on Social Media

What this basically means is that everything and anything you share to social media, whether that be words, photos, videos, or some other form of content, can never be truly erased from internet, and it can always be linked back to you. This is because everything that is shared online is documented by multiple sources, and you cannot control these sources. For instance, if you were to post a picture on Facebook, every single one of your Facebook friends could potentially see this picture, and could save the picture if they so wanted to. If you later on decided to delete the picture, it would be removed from your profile. However, anyone who might have originally saw the posted picture could have documented that you posted it, and they possibly could have saved the picture. Thus, that person could have a record that you indeed did post the photo.

> **Best Practice:** Before making any type of post to social media, always keep in mind that whatever you post can never truly be deleted.

A Private Social Media Profile is not truly private

Many social media platforms allow you to add some privacy features to your profile. For instance, Facebook allows you to customize your profile so that only your Facebook friends can see what you post. Twitter and Instagram also allow you to customize your profile so that only your approved followers can see your content. Unfortunately, this does not change the fact that anything and everything you post on these private social media accounts will be available to the public forever. This is because your Facebook friends or profile followers can always share what you post with other people, or simply document what you posted with a screenshot.

> **Best Practice:** A private social media account is still susceptible to having its information become public. Therefore, you should treat all of your social media profiles as if everyone in the public can see its information.

Private Messages you send on Social Media are not as private as you think

Nearly all social media platforms allow you to send private or direct messages to other people through its platform. It is true that only you and the person you are sending the message to can see the messages, but that does not mean that your messages are completely secure. People have their social media accounts hacked all the time, often through phishing scams such as the ones covered in Chapter 4. If someone's social media account gets hacked, that means the hacker can potentially see and even share all of their private messages on that platform. Therefore, you should take great caution when exchanging private messages with someone over social media, and keep in mind that those messages could potentially be exposed.

> **Best Practice:** If you want to make sure your private messages exchanged through social media are kept safe and secure, make sure the people you are conversing with are well-versed on online safety. If they are not, buy them this book.

Your Specific Activity on Social Media can be exposed under Certain Circumstances

Generally, your browsing activity on social media is confidential and is kept secure by the social media platform. Your browsing activity includes which profiles you are looking at, what articles you are reading, and whatever else you are doing on the platform. However, law enforcement agencies in certain jurisdictions can sometimes obtain your browsing information through lawful methods, such as subpoenas and warrants. Furthermore, some social media platforms keep a history of your browsing activity, which could potentially be exposed if your account was ever hacked. Therefore, you should always keep in mind that your social media activity is never truly private.

The #1 Rule of Social Media will help you make better decisions when deciding what to share on social media, and will help keep you safe now and in the future. If you are ever in doubt on whether to post something on a social media platform, always err on the side of caution and think about the #1 rule.

Remember, the #1 rule of social media is: **There is no such thing as privacy when using social media, and anything you share on social media will <u>forever</u> will be public.**

Internet Trolls

An internet troll is an anonymous person whose sole purpose online is to cause some sort of strife. They often use a fake name and fake profile picture, and are often posting information meant to get under people's skin and create arguments. Social media and the internet in general are filled with these trolls, and it is important for you to be able to recognize them so you can save yourself from a potential headache, especially if you decide to engage with a troll. Most of the time an internet troll can be easily identified, and here is what you can look for:

Common Characteristics of an Internet Troll

- Does not use a real name to identify their profile
- Does not have a profile picture or their profile picture does not show a real person
- Oftentimes their profile only has one personal photo or no photos at all
- They have a relatively small number or social media friends or followers
- Their social media activity is filled with troll-like comments and posts

Here is an example of a troll. Let's say you are a member of a Facebook group about gardening, and you decide to create a post showing a photo of the new tomatoes your garden has spawned. You write in your post about how you plan to use the tomatoes in the dinner you are cooking tonight, and your family is excited to eat them. Your post gets some likes and the comments are generally friendly, however one person comments, *"This is disgusting. Tomatoes are a living thing with feelings too, and eating tomatoes should be a crime. I hope the tomatoes fight back and make you sick."* This comment may seem completely ludicrous and downright laughable, but the internet troll thrives on outrage and shock, and in this case they are just hoping for someone to respond to their comment so they can come back with even more ridiculous replies.

In the grand scheme of things, internet trolls are mostly harmless. They enjoy creating arguments and getting reactions from people online. It is completely up to you if you want to engage with trolls online (some people actually enjoy doing so), but you should understand that you will be engaging with an anonymous person who is just trying to get under your or someone else's skin. It is also pertinent to understand that trolls often travel in packs. So if you start arguing with one troll, that troll may get his troll friends to harass and bother you online. My advice: if you encounter a troll online that is bothering you, simply ignore them. If the troll starts to target you specifically, block them. Lastly, if the troll starts harassing you or gets other trolls to harass you, report the troll to the social media platform.

Facebook Safety

Facebook is the biggest social media platform on the planet. Fortunately, they have some of the best security features to keep you safe and they are constantly improving these features. However, their safeguards cannot protect you or your children from all threats, so in the following sections I will educate you on the best practices you can follow to be safe when using Facebook.

Facebook: Common Scams

There are a number of scams that scammers commonly attempt on people on Facebook. In this section I will show you how these scams work, and what you can do to protect yourself from them.

The Unknown Friend Request – Sex Appeal

This is a very common scam that you have probably seen before if you use Facebook. The way this scam starts is with a friend request from someone you do not know. The request will usually come from someone of the opposite sex, and that someone is usually attractive and wearing attractive clothes in their profile picture. This scam is also more common if you are a man. Once you accept the friend request, the person who befriended you may try to contact you through a private message and attempt to start a conversation. The conversation will be light at first, and eventually the person will attempt to seduce you through the private messages. Their final goal will be to try and get you to sign up for some website or service in order for you to keep talking with them. The way this works is they will usually send you a link and ask you to go to that website and sign up for something, such as a "verification service" so they know that you a real person and not dangerous. This is a complete scam and they are just trying to get your money.

You can defend yourself in this situation in a few different ways. First, whenever you receive a friend request from someone you do not know, you should look at their Facebook profile first before accepting the request. When looking at their profile, you want to try and surmise whether this person is real and whether they use their profile in a genuine way. So to check for this, I would suggest looking at their pictures, starting with their profile picture. The first thing you want to see is if that they have multiple photos, which if they do, is a good sign. Then, you want to make sure that they actually appear in more than one photo. If they are only in one photo and the rest of the photos do not contain themselves or people in general, then you may be dealing with a fake account. If they do appear in multiple photos, then that is a positive sign that the person is indeed real.

If you do decide to accept a friend request from someone you do not know, then you should consider private messaging them to ask why they are sending you a friend request. Their response, if they even send one, will help you determine if their intentions are genuine.

The "Need Help" Post

This scam is particularly shameful as it plays on people's desire to help people in need. The way this scam works is a person will either contact you directly or post to a Facebook group a short story about their struggles. Near the end of their story, they will ask for a small *direct payment to themselves* to help them get through the situation. Now, it is perfectly plausible that the person is indeed in need of financial help and is seriously asking for assistance, however I have found that the vast majority of the time the people making these requests on Facebook are being disingenuous and are out to make as much money as they can off as many people as they can. So in this situation how can we tell the difference between a genuine request and a scammer?

There are a couple of different things you can look at. The first thing you should look at is where they want you to send the money. If in their post they ask you to send the money directly to them through an app or service such as Venmo, Cash app, PayPal, or Patreon, then that is a red flag that they are just fishing for free money. On the other hand, if they are providing a link to a well-known charity, then that may be acceptable. The second thing worth checking is if they have posted in multiple Facebook groups, which is another red flag. The last thing worth looking at is the responses from other people who have seen the post. When someone makes a post like this, others will typically chime in and provide information on whether the person is really in need or not.

The Official Request for Information

This scam typically starts with a friend request from an unknown person. Then, after you accept the friend request, this person will usually send you a private message indicating they are an official with some organization or government, and they need your personal information for some reason. This is a complete scam and you should never give out your private information to a stranger on social media, especially through private messaging.

Facebook: Friends & Friend Requests

As you may have noticed, two of the three common Facebook scams covered started with a friend request from someone you do not know. The reason these scammers send a friend request first is because they need to be Facebook friends with you in order to send you a direct message that you will see. One of Facebook's security features is to hide direct messages you receive from people who are not your friends. Being able to deal with friend requests from unknown persons is an important aspect of keeping yourself safe while using Facebook.

Friend Request from Someone you do not know

A friend request from someone you do not know can be completely harmless. Many people use Facebook to meet new friends, and the person sending you a friend request could have found you through a group or through some post they saw you make. It is completely up to you whether you want to accept a friend request from a stranger. Just know that by accepting a friend request, that person will be able to see your full profile and write you messages.

On the other hand, if you only want to accept friend requests from people you might know, then you should always look to see how many mutual friends you share. Whenever you receive a friend request, Facebook will tell you how many mutual friends you share when you view their profile.

Facebook: Private Messages

With Facebook, you have the ability to send and receive private messages with other Facebook users using the messaging service called Facebook Messenger. By default, Facebook will hide messages you receive from people who are not your friends as a security precaution. This is an excellent security feature which protects you from receiving spam and phishing attacks. There are also some additional safety aspects worth noting.

Secret Conversations

Facebook Messenger allows you to create and hold secret conversations with other users, which are encrypted from end-to-end. In other words, nobody, not even Facebook or the government could access these messages without first getting access to your account. If security and privacy are a major concern for you, then I recommend you use secret conversations when using Facebook Messenger. Although these messages are encrypted, you should still remember that the #1 Rule of Social Media still applies.

Facebook: Best Practices

In general, Facebook is a very safe social media platform to use. Facebook has many automated security features that protect you from harmful content. For instance, if someone posts a well-known dangerous link (such as a fraudulent website), Facebook will automatically block the person from posting the link, and may even suspend the individual's account. Their security is not 100% foolproof, so you should always be aware of potential risks when encountering any suspicious content. Follow these best practices to have a safe and reliable Facebook experience.

> **Best Practice:** Never share your financial information to any Facebook group, event, or profile page. This includes your credit card and payment details. If you must share your financial data with a company or person, only do so using Facebook Messenger and even then, use extra caution.

Facebook does allow you to shop using their platform, so using a credit card on a company Facebook page is generally safe and secure. However, you should never post your financial information to any public space on Facebook that can be easily read by other members of the public.

> **Best Practice:** Never share any of your passwords through Facebook Messenger. Never post any of your passwords to any Facebook group or page.

Facebook Messenger is a secure messaging service, however it is always good policy to never share any of your passwords with any person or entity.

> **Best Practice:** Use Facebook's Privacy Shortcuts to control your privacy and security on Facebook.

Facebook has many privacy and security controls, known as Privacy Shortcuts, which allow you to customize all of the privacy aspects of your Facebook account and profile. With these shortcuts, you can choose who can see your profile, who can contact you, and more. To access these Privacy Shortcuts, on a computer, login to Facebook and go to Settings and then Privacy (Figure 5.1).

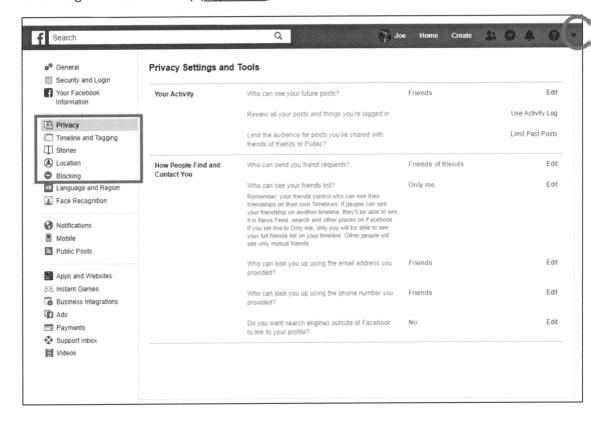

Figure 5.1 – Accessing Facebook's Privacy Settings on a Computer

On a mobile device, open the Facebook app, tap on the Menu icon, tap on <u>Settings & Privacy</u>, and then tap on <u>Privacy Shortcuts</u> (<u>Figure 5.2</u>).

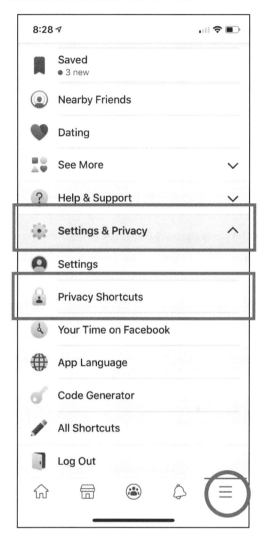

Figure 5.2 – Accessing Facebook's Privacy Settings on a Mobile Device

Here are some of the privacy options you can customize: (<u>Figures 5.3 – 5.5</u>)

This option will take you through a walkthrough of some of the most important privacy settings on Facebook

Customize more privacy settings

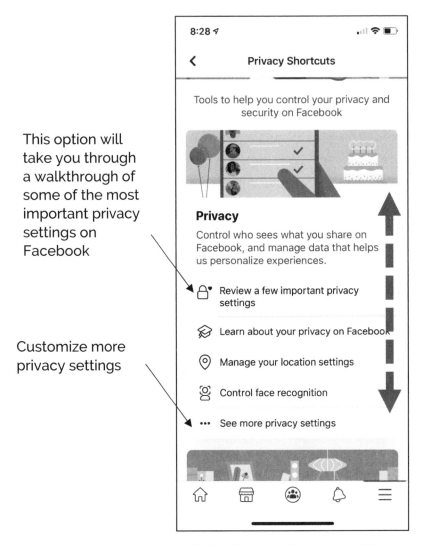

Figure 5.3 – Privacy Shortcuts of Facebook

By selecting <u>See more privacy settings</u> in <u>Figure 5.3</u>, you can alter some the following privacy options (<u>Figure 5.4</u>):

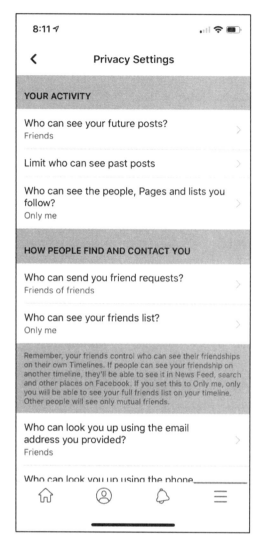

Figure 5.4 – Privacy Settings of Facebook

<u>Who can see your future posts</u> – This allows you to change who can see all of your future posts. You can change this to friends only, everyone, certain people, or just yourself.

<u>Limit who can see past posts</u> – With this option, you can change all of your past posts so that only your friends or currently selected option can see them.

<u>Who can see the people, Pages, and lists you follow</u> – This option allows you to customize who can see certain information on your profile, such as the people and

pages you follow. You can set this Public (everyone), friends, certain people, or just yourself.

Who can send you friend requests – This option lets you limit who can send you a friend request. You can set this to everyone or friends of friends. Settings this to friends of friends will help prevent scammers and predators from sending you friend requests.

Who can see your friends list – Decide who you want to be able to see your friends list on your profile. You can set this to everyone, friends, certain friends, or just yourself. When you set this to just yourself, nobody but you will be able to see your friends list.

Do you want search engines outside of Facebook to link to your profile – This option allows you to hide your Facebook profile from search engines such as Bing and Google. When this option is set to yes, if someone searches for your name on a search engine, your Facebook profile may appear.

Here are some account security options you can customize by scrolling down on the Privacy Shortcuts screen (Figure 5.5):

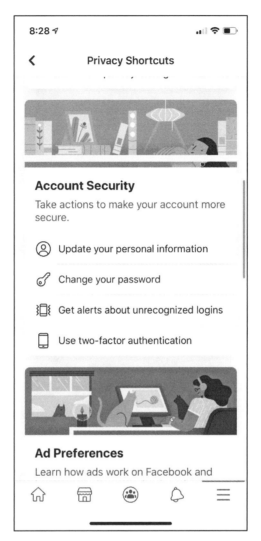

Figure 5.5 – Account Security Settings of Facebook

Change your password – Allows you to change your Facebook password. If you ever suspect your Facebook account is compromised, you should immediately change your password.

Use two-factor authentication – Allows you to setup two-factor authentication for your Facebook account, which means in addition to your password, you will need to pass another layer of security to access your account, such as text message verification.

Here are some Facebook information options you can control (Figure 5.6):

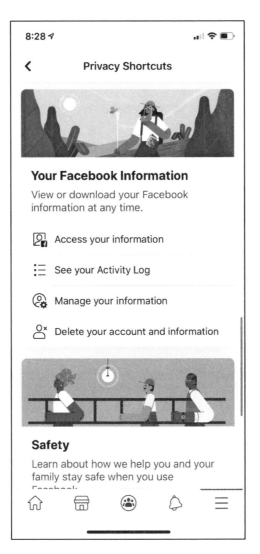

Figure 5.6 – View your Facebook Information

See your Activity Log – Lets you see the history of your activity on Facebook, including which profiles you have visited, any posts you have made, and any posts you have liked.

Delete your account and information – Allows you to delete your Facebook account and all data associated with it.

Best Practice: Facebook is one of the safest social media platforms to use, but you should have a good understanding of how to use Facebook and its features in order to use it safely. If you need some training on using Facebook, visit www.infinityguides.com and watch the Facebook for Beginners course.

Twitter Safety

Twitter (www.twitter.com) is another popular social media platform where you can send out public posts, called tweets, to your followers. A tweet is a character limited post that can contain text, images, photos, videos, and links. Also with Twitter, you can follow friends, celebrities, companies, and important individuals to keep up with their activity. Compared with Facebook, Twitter is a more open-oriented platform that encourages short snippets of dialogue and piquant responses.

Twitter: Warnings

Twitter explicitly allows content that many other social media platforms do not, including bots and pornography, with the latter being something you can easily shield yourself from. A bot on Twitter is a computer generated account that automatically performs actions, such as tweeting, following users, and sending messages. Many of these bots are extremely entertaining and useful, such as weather bots that report weather information or crime bots that report crime data. Other bots can be a little annoying, such as ones that constantly post links to try and advertise something.

Pornography is also allowed on Twitter. You will only see pornography on Twitter if you follow accounts that post it. Otherwise, you should never see pornography on the platform unless you seek it out. If you do inadvertently come across pornography while using Twitter and you do not want to see it, you should immediately block the account.

You are also likely to see profanity on Twitter, and there is little you can do to avoid it.

Twitter: Following & Followers

On your Twitter profile, you will have a followers and a following section. Your followers are other Twitter users who follow your profile, and will therefore see everything you tweet. Your following section is a list of profiles that you follow, and you will see their tweets on your home Twitter page, known as your Twitter feed. If you set your profile to public, anyone can follow you and see your Twitter profile along with all of your tweets. If you set your profile to private, you can choose who you allow to follow your profile, and your tweets will only be seen by those approved followers. Therefore, if you want to maintain a semi-private Twitter profile, I suggest you set your profile to private. If on the other hand you want a fully public Twitter profile or want to use your account for promotion, I suggest setting your profile to public.

Whether you set your Twitter profile to public or private, the #1 Rule of Social Media still applies. Another important aspect to consider is that everyone can see which profiles you follow. So if you plan to follow some profiles that you would rather not have anyone know about, then you might not want to use your real name when creating your Twitter account.

Twitter: Direct Messages

The private messaging system for Twitter is known as direct messages (DMs). DMs are a great way to privately communicate with other Twitter users, and are also a great way for scammers and predators to contact you. You should use caution whenever you receive a DM from someone you do not know, and always use extreme caution when someone sends you a link through a direct message. If you would like, you can set your profile to only receive DMs from people you follow by altering the privacy and safety option inside your Twitter account's settings.

Twitter: Tweets & Links

Twitter is a simple social media platform that is dominated by tweets. A tweet is simply a post from a Twitter user and it can be text, photos, videos, links, or a combination of these. Most links posted on Twitter are in a shortened form, so you may have trouble seeing exactly where the link leads to. Fortunately, for most links Twitter will show a preview of the link's content inside a tweet, such as a brief synopsis of the webpage, a picture, and the link's true URL (Figure 5.7).

Links posted in tweets can sometimes appear as a preview of the web page. The domain of the link will be shown inside this preview so you can easily verify where the link will be directing you to.

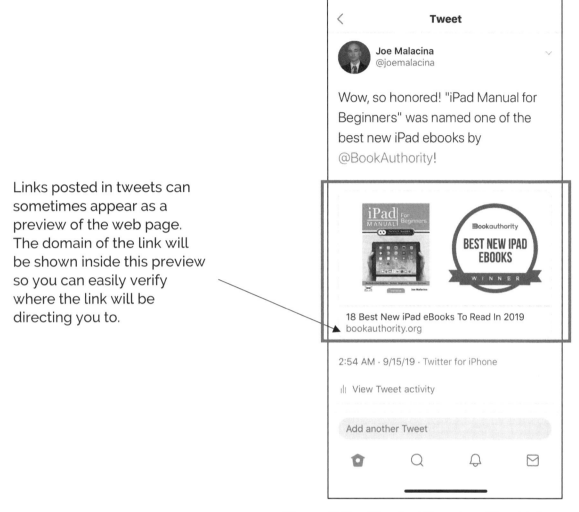

Figure 5.7 – Viewing Tweets with a Link

If you are going to be using Twitter and clicking on links, then you should familiarize yourself with Chapter 2 and Chapter 7, as these chapters will teach you the basics in online web browsing.

Twitter: Common Scams

Twitter scams appear in two main forms: tweets and direct messages. For the tweets, an anonymous Twitter profile will post a link publicly usually offering some too good to be true promise, such as "Click this link to win $500". Then after you click on the link you are brought to a web page that solicits your information, which of course you should refuse to enter. Most tweet scams appear in this way in one form or another, which is why it is so important for you to understand the basic web browsing safety principles and best practices covered in Chapter 2 and later in Chapter 7.

For direct message scams, these are more like the Facebook Messenger scams. The way this works is a Twitter user will send you a direct message, and more times than not, the Twitter user is anonymous and is using a fake account. The user will start a friendly conversation and slowly try to fool you into believing who they are. Eventually, the conversation will proceed to the user posting a link and asking you to click on it. The link will direct you to a website that asks you to disclose your financial or sensitive information. As always, treat direct messages you receive in this form as suspicious and follow the best practices preached in Chapter 2 to protect yourself from harm.

Twitter: Safety Features

Twitter has a number of built-in safety features that you can customize to better control your safety and security. These features are not foolproof, but will go a long way in keeping you safe while using the platform.

To access these safety features, open the Settings feature in Twitter and click on Privacy and Safety.

Here inside Privacy and Safety you can customize some options (Figure 5.8):

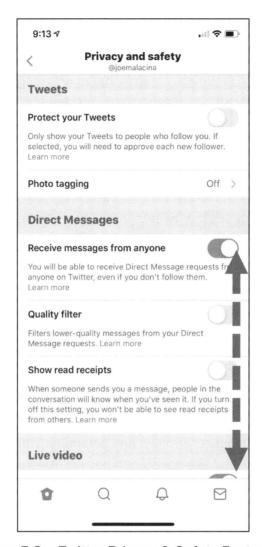

Figure 5.8 – Twitter Privacy & Safety Features

Protect your Tweets – Enabling this option will set your Twitter profile to private which means that only your followers can view your tweets, and you will need to manually approve each new follower for the future.

Quality filter – Enabling this option will prevent you from receiving harmful direct messages such as spam, phishing, and advertisements.

Display media that may contain sensitive content – Checking this box will remove all filters that Twitter uses to hide sensitive content, such as pornography, from appearing on your feed. When this is unchecked, Twitter will do its best to hide pornography and other sensitive content from ever appearing on your feed.

Mark media you Tweet as containing material that may be sensitive – If you use your Twitter account to tweet sensitive content, then you should check this box. This will hide your tweets from appearing on people's feeds who do not want to see sensitive content.

Muted – This option allows you to mute accounts and words from your feed. When an account is muted, you will not see any of their tweets on your feed. When you mute a word or phrase, you will not see any tweets that contain these words or phrases on your feed.

Blocked accounts – When you block an account, you will not be able to see any of their tweets or profile information, and they will not be able to see yours. They also will not be able to tweet you or send you direct messages.

Best Practice: There are many online trolls on Twitter. Use the block function frequently and indiscriminately when you come across trolls who harass you.

Twitter: Best Practices

Twitter can be a very fun, entertaining, and informational social media platform. It is great for finding specific accounts to follow and communicating with them. Twitter can also get a little chaotic and its users can sometimes act like a mob. If you are completely new to Twitter and want to learn how to use it, watch the online Twitter course at www.infinityguides.com.

Best Practice: Customize your Twitter Safety features in Settings to fit your needs.

Instagram Safety

Instagram (Figure 5.9) is a social media platform owned by Facebook where users share photos and short video clips to their followers. Their followers can then like or comment on their posts. It is an extremely popular social media platform, especially for the younger generations. If you are a parent with a child in high school, there is a very good chance that your child uses Instagram. Instagram is mainly used on mobile phones through its app, although you can use it on a computer as well.

Instagram is a tightly controlled and organized platform; there is no pornography allowed and no clickable links can be shared on a post. Furthermore, the amount of text allowed on posts and comments is character limited. There is also no native way to save other people's posted photos and videos. Because of Instagram's rigid controls and features, it is a very safe app to use for most users. Many of the safety risks involved with using Instagram come from direct messages from other users, and we will cover these risks shortly.

Figure 5.9 – Instagram App (Profile View)

Instagram: Your Profile, Followers, & Following

Like Twitter, with Instagram you can choose to set your profile to public or private. When set to public, anyone can view your posts and anyone can follow you. If you set your profile to private, only your followers can see your posts and you can manually approve who you allow to follow you. When you follow a profile, you will see their posts on your feed. If you try to follow a private account, that user must accept your follow request in order for you to see their posts.

When deciding who to follow, keep in mind that others can see who you are following. If you profile is public, everyone can see who you are following along with who is following you. If your profile is private, only your followers can see this information.

The Increase your Followers Scam

A common scam seen on Instagram is the increase your followers scam. Many people use Instagram for self-promotion, so increasing your follower count is crucial to reaching a bigger audience. There are many people out there who try and take advantage of this fact by offering to sell you a large number of followers. The way it works is usually someone will send you a direct message offering to get you hundreds or thousands of followers for a fee. There is no way to tell if what they are offering is real, and the majority of the time they are just trying to scam you. Not only this, but purchasing followers may go against Instagram's terms of service, which could result in action being taken against your account. So if you receive a shady message from someone offering to sell you followers, ignore the message or block them.

This is different from other follower increasing tactics that are perfectly legitimate and allowed by Instagram. It is common for someone to follow you in the hopes that you will follow them back; they may even ask you to do so. It is also common for someone to ask you to give their profile a shot-out in the hopes that they will gain more followers in exchange for doing the same for you (you can do this by mentioning their username in one of your posts with the @username tag). Both of these practices are completely acceptable and a great way to increase the number of followers for your profile.

Instagram: Direct Messages

Direct messages on Instagram is the best and only way to have a private conversation with someone or a group of people on the app. You can also use direct messages to share other Instagram posts you come across with your friends. Just like with direct messages on Twitter, you should always exercise caution when you receive a direct message from someone you do not know, especially if it contains a link.

Instagram: Safety Features

Instagram has a few safety features that you can access through the app's settings. These features include the ability to block accounts, mute accounts, and filter comments. If you block an account, that account will not be able to see your profile at all, including your posts. They also will not be able to contact you on Instagram. When you mute an account, then you will not see any of their posts or comments appear on your feed. Lastly, you can filter comments to hide offensive content such as profanity and sexual language. When filtering comments, Instagram will do its best to make sure you do not see offensive comments on posts you are viewing.

Instagram: Best Practices

Instagram is a very safe social media platform compared to others. Your biggest risk comes from people contacting you through direct messages and trying to scam you. Your only exposure to clickable links on Instagram is either in direct messages or when viewing someone's profile information (they are allowed to post one link in the description of their profile, as are you [See <u>Figure 5.9</u>]).

> **Best Practice:** Always use caution when someone you do not know contacts you through a direct message on Instagram.

> **Best Practice:** If you have children who use Instagram, read the Instagram section in Chapter 9 about the different type of threats they are prone to.

Snapchat Safety

Snapchat is a unique social media platform only available as a mobile app. With Snapchat, you can send and receive photos, videos, and messages directly to other users. The catch is, these photos and videos can only be viewed once and will disappear after a short amount of time. Once a received photo or video disappears from you, you can generally never see it again. The way this works is when you send a live photo to someone on Snapchat, you can choose how long you want the content to appear. Once the allotted time runs out, the photo or video will disappear.

In order to understand the safety risks of using Snapchat, we need to explore a little deeper the ways in which the app works. Here are some defining aspects of Snapchat:

- Disappearing photos and videos generally must be sent live, meaning to send one of these you must take the photo or video right now, and then immediately send it to someone on Snapchat. A photo or video you already have saved usually cannot be sent with the disappearing feature.

- You can also send direct messages to people on Snapchat. These messages will disappear after the recipient reads them **only if** they choose not to save the message.
- Users on Snapchat can create and post stories, which are collections of various posts they have made throughout the day. These stories will be available for all of their friends to see for 24 hours, and they can be viewed as many times as they would like.
- When you send a photo or video to someone, known as sending a *snap*, you can choose how long you want that content to be shown on the recipient's screen. You can choose between 1 and 10 seconds, or indefinitely, in which case the recipient can view the snap as long as they keep it open.
- Snapchat is extremely popular among the younger generations, especially teenagers and young adults.

Snapchat: Warnings

The promises of Snapchat seem too good to be true: send and receive live photos and videos to someone (called sending and receiving snaps) with no lasting consequences, since whatever you send will disappear after a set amount of time and never be allowed to be seen again. Luckily, you have been reading this book, you already know that the #1 Rule of Social Media always remains true, even for an app like Snapchat. **There is no such thing as privacy when using social media, and anything you share on social media will <u>forever</u> will be public**. Repeat that sentence in your head, and if you have children who use social media make sure they understand it as well. The internet never forgets, and Snapchat is no different when it comes to the #1 Rule.

How can this be? How is it that the #1 Rule of Social Media remains true when every photo or video you send on Snapchat deletes itself after a few seconds? It's simple really, when it comes to the internet there is always a way to get around restrictions, and here is how it is commonly done on Snapchat.

The first and most obvious way around the disappearing *snap* feature of Snapchat is a screenshot. Anyone can easily take a screenshot of whatever they are viewing on their smartphone and save it as a picture in as little as one second. So any snap you send to someone can be screenshotted by the recipient and that photo could forever be saved. Interestingly enough, Snapchat will notify you if someone screenshots a snap you have sent, so you will know if someone screenshotted a picture that you did not want saved, if that's any consolation.

Another way someone can get around the disappearing feature of Snapchat is by simply recording the snap using another device. In this case, there is no way of knowing that a recipient has saved your snap. This can easily be done by using another phone or camera and recording the screen of the device used to view the snap.

Lastly, Snapchat has a feature that allows users to see a snap again! Typically, this feature can only be used once per day and if someone does use it, the sender of the snap will be notified that the person viewed it again. So if the recipient wants to permanently save the snap you sent them, they have a second chance to do so.

So what does all of this tell us? It tells us that anything you send on Snapchat can potentially be saved and made public. Is also tells us that if you are going to be sending photos or videos through Snapchat that you never want to be made public, then you should only send those to people you completely trust. Unfortunately, many people have had learn this the hard way by having their private photos they sent over Snapchat be later shared with the public.

Snapchat: Friends

With the Snapchat app, you can add friends to your account by adding their username. You can also search your contact list to add friends that have associated their Snapchat account with their phone number. This allows you to easily find friends to converse with over the app. Other Snapchat users can also find you if you share a mutual friend.

On occasion, you may receive a friend request from someone you do not recognize. This is somewhat normal as snap usernames often share no resemblance to a person's real name. Some people also purposefully do not associate their real name with their Snapchat account, and it will be up to you to determine if you know the person. If you start receiving snaps from someone you do not want to converse with, you can easily block them.

Snapchat: Private Messages

The private messages feature of Snapchat is different than sending a live photo or video to someone. The main feature of private messages is the ability to have a text conversation, or "chat". The catch is, any messages you send to someone over private message will delete itself after it has been read, **unless** the recipient decides to save it. In this case, the person does not have to take a screenshot or record their device; they can simply use the Snapchat save feature to save the message. Furthermore, any photos or videos you send over private messages can be easily saved by the recipient through the same feature. Therefore, do not expect any disappearing privacy when using private messages.

Snapchat: Risks

Snapchat is susceptible to certain safety risks just like any other social media platform. One such risk is when you are using private messages with someone you do not know personally. If that person directs you to click on a link or visit a webpage, you should exercise caution and use the best practices covered in Chapter 2.

The other big "risk" you should be aware is the so called "premium Snapchat". Technically, there is no such thing as a premium Snapchat account but this practice is often seen throughout the platform by certain users. The way it works is someone, typically an amateur adult entertainer or X-rated model, will have a public Snapchat account that posts revealing, but technically not sexually explicit content. In addition, this account will then have in their snaps or Snapchat story information about their *premium Snapchat*, which they will claim is completely uncensored and only available to certain users who request access. Naturally, in order to get access to this person's premium account, payment is required, and the person will usually provide information on how you can pay them and get access to their premium account through a private message.

First and foremost, nudity and sexually explicit content is forbidden by Snapchat's Terms of Service. However, that does not mean that it does not occur. Any account caught sharing this forbidden content could be banned from using Snapchat, and people who view their "premium content" could also face consequences. The concept of a premium Snapchat without nudity or sexually explicit content itself may technically not be against Snapchat's terms of service, however you would be hard-pressed to find a *premium Snapchat* account that was not sexual in nature. Therefore, you should be aware that if you come across someone on Snapchat offering a *premium Snapchat*, there is a good chance that the account in question is associated with sexually explicit content.

Snapchat: Best Practices

Snapchat is a relatively safe social media platform when used properly. You should always use caution when conversing with people you do not know, especially if that person directs you to a link or asks for a payment of some sort. Furthermore, Snapchat has a blocking feature in which you can completely block accounts that are troubling you. Most importantly, you must remember that the #1 Rule of Social Media still applies for Snapchat, even though it has the disappearing feature.

> **Best Practice:** Always remember the #1 Rule of Social Media when using Snapchat. Everything you send or say on Snapchat could potentially become public, and there is no sure-fire way to guarantee that what you send remains completely private.

General Best Practices of Social Media

So far we have covered the most popular social media platforms of the day and the specific safety aspects worth considering for each of them. Many of the best practices stated throughout this chapter will work on every social media platform, especially the ones related to direct/private messages. We will close out this chapter with some general best practices that will work for most social media platforms, including platforms that were not mentioned such as Pinterest, LinkedIn, and Tumblr.

General Best Practice 1: To Use a Real or Fake Name

When creating an account for a social media platform, you may find yourself wondering if you should use your real name or use an online identity (an online identity is just an identity or nickname you create for yourself that does not relay your personal information in any way.) The answer comes down to which social media platform you are using, and what you plan to use it for. Some social media platforms require that you use your real name, while others allow anonymity. Keep in mind that for certain platforms, other people can see who you follow and who your friends are. If you want to hide this type of information, make sure you use a private account (if applicable) or use an online identity. If you do decide to use your online identity instead of your real name for a social media platform, you should make sure that you do not use your normal phone number with that account since many platforms use that number to help your friends find your profile.

General Naming Practices & Requirements per Platform

- Facebook: Requires that you use your real name
- LinkedIn: Requires that you use your real name
- Twitter: Use your real name if you plan on promoting yourself or want to interact with your friends on Twitter. Use your online identity if you want complete anonymity on Twitter.
- Instagram: Use your real name if you plan to follow your friends and family, and posts personal photos. Use your online identity if you want complete anonymity.
- Snapchat: Use your real name if plan to interact with your friends and family, and use an online identity if you want to remain anonymous.

87

General Best Practice 2: Review your Account History Periodically

This best practice can save you from potential headaches later on. If you have had a social media account for a while, such as a Facebook or Twitter account, it is worth going back and looking at your history every now and then to see if there is anything you want to delete. There may be some pictures that are unflattering or posts that are now insensitive that you may want to delete so the public cannot see them. Sadly, we live in a society where something you said on social media 20 years ago can come back to bite you in serious ways, so following this best practice can save you from falling victim to this sort of thing.

General Best Practice 3: Take a Break from Social Media at Regular Intervals

This best practice does not have much to do with online safety, but it is worth following. Research has shown that social media can be addictive for some people, and overuse of social media can lead to emotional problems such as depression. My advice is simple: if you find yourself using social media every day, try to have one day a week where you do not use social media at all. You may find that you enjoy these days off from social media more than your days on.

Chapter 6 – Mobile Device Safety

Mobile devices are devices that you can carry with you and work just like any computer. The two main types of mobile devices are smartphones and tablets, with smartphones being the most popular. Some common smartphones include the Apple iPhone, Samsung Galaxy, HTC One, and Google Pixel. Common tablets include the Apple iPad, Samsung Galaxy Tab, Amazon Fire HD, and Microsoft Surface. Each of these devices work in very similar ways and share the same risks when it comes to online safety. Fortunately, everything we have covered in the first five chapters applies to both mobile devices and computers, so you can apply everything you have learned so far to your mobile device as well. In this chapter, we will explore some specific safety aspects of using smartphones and tablets that are important for you to know.

Safety of Different Brands

If you are shopping for a mobile device such as a smartphone or tablet, then it would be prudent for you to appreciate the reputations of different brands and the built-in safety features they are known for. Here is my personal rundown of the different brands:

Apple

Apple is the creator of the famous iPhone and iPad, and their devices are notorious for being extremely safe and reliable. Furthermore, Apple takes the privacy of its customers seriously, and their devices go above and beyond their competitors in protecting your sensitive and non-sensitive information. For instance, the software that runs on the iPhone and iPad is tightly controlled, which makes it very difficult for malicious software or hackers to penetrate and access your data. Furthermore, their devices use high level encryption to protect nearly every aspect of the device, including iMessages (which are text messages sent to and from Apple devices). To see how serious they are about their privacy practices, look no further than the United States' case in 2016 in which the Federal Bureau of Investigation (FBI) tried desperately to access an alleged terrorist's iPhone, and they struggled greatly trying to accomplish this. They eventually did get in to the amazement of everyone, but the example shows just how secure Apple mobile devices are.

Furthermore, Apple has a tightly controlled app marketplace that protects its users from potentially being exposed to fraudulent apps. In order for a developer to list an app on Apple's App Store, it must go through a rigorous approval process. In my opinion, Apple has the most disciplined app marketplace compared to others.

Samsung

Samsung is one of the largest smartphone and tablet makers in the world. Their devices typically use the Android operating system, which is designed by Google. The Android system is a safe and reliable operating system, however, Android devices have been known to be more vulnerable to hackers and malicious apps. This is simply because Android is an open-source system, which means that users and manufacturers can alter some of the code, which further means there are more opportunities for hackers to find a vulnerability. Android devices are also targeted for attack more often than Apple devices simply because the Android operating system is more widely used throughout the world compared to others.

These vulnerabilities do not necessarily make the Android operating system unsafe to use. As long as you use your mobile device in a safe and secure manner by following the best practices in this book, you will be well on your way to protecting yourself from a hacker or scammer.

Google

Google is the designer of the Pixel smartphone as well as the Android operating system. The Android operating system is the most widely used operating system on mobile devices, and its safety aspects are well noted. The Google brand is well-known for innovation and for its ecosystem. For instance, when you use a device with the Android operating system, it is very easy to access and use many of Google's products such as Gmail, Google Talk, and Google Drive. So if you rely heavily on using Google's products and services, you may want to consider using a device that utilizes the Android operating system.

Amazon

Amazon currently does not make smartphones, but they do make the popular Fire tablets, Kindle electronic readers, and Alexa devices. Many of their devices utilize the Fire OS operating system, which is an Android based system. Therefore, many of the safety aspects discussed in the Google section apply to Amazon devices as well. Amazon devices work great within the Amazon ecosystem; so if you find yourself using a lot of Amazon devices and services, you may want to consider an Amazon product for your newest mobile device.

Mobile Web Browsing

Nearly every mobile device allows you to access the internet and surf the web. When surfing the web on a mobile device, the same rules apply as if you were surfing the web on a computer (see Chapter 2). Furthermore, there are some additional things to watch out for when web surfing on a mobile device.

Choose Your Web Browser and Stick with It

Every mobile device comes with a default web browser. For Apple devices, the default browser is Safari. For Samsung and Google devices, the default browser is either Google Chrome or the Internet app. For Amazon, the default web browser is Silk. In addition, there are several other web browsers you can download from your device's app store, such as Firefox, Microsoft Edge, and Brave. Whichever browser you decide to use to surf the web, you should stick with that browser for all of your other mobile devices. This is because your web browser will save your passwords and login information for you (if you so choose), making it easier for you to login and visit your favorite websites. These browsers will also save your security and privacy settings so you will not have to deal with different settings when switching devices.

For more information on the different web browsers available, please see Chapter 2.

Privacy Concerns

As covered in Chapter 2, many websites track your data and share that data with other websites and systems. In turn, advertising systems use this data to deliver you relevant advertisements while you browse the web. If this practice concerns you, you can use the private browsing feature on your web browser to limit the data websites can gather from you. Nearly every web browser has this feature, and each browser has a different name for it (Figure 6.1):

- Safari - Private Browsing
- Chrome - Incognito Browsing
- Edge - InPrivate Browsing
- Brave - Private Browsing

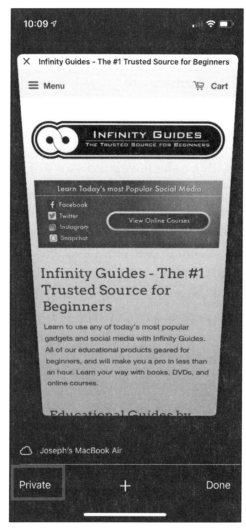

Figure 6.1 – Private Browsing on a Mobile Web Browser (Safari on iPhone shown)

You can find the private browsing mode on most mobile web browsers either by opening a new tab or by tapping the options icon.

General Web Browsing Safety

For all other mobile web browsing safety aspects and best practices, please read Chapter 2.

Texting & Messaging Safety

Text messaging is a very common form of communication, and is part and parcel of owning a mobile device. When texting your friends, family members, and people you know, there is little risk to your safety as cellular texting devices are very secure against unwanted intrusions. However, when you receive a text message from someone you do not know, there are multiple safety aspects to consider.

Automated Text Messages

The first type of text message from an unknown sender you are bound to receive is an automated text message from a company or service. These text messages are popular as alerts and for security purposes. An example of this is a text message from your bank whenever you make a withdrawal over $100. Another example is a text message from a company providing you a two-factor authentication code or a forgotten password code. These are completely normal text messages if you signed up for them and are commonly used to provide you with a better service. With that said, some scammers take advantage of this practice to try and fool you into revealing your passwords or financial information. So let's examine the different types of automated text messages and the best practices that accompany them.

Two-Factor Authentication Code

Two-factor authentication codes are an additional layer of security to protect any of your online accounts. Here is how it works step by step:

1. You go to a website or app where you have two-factor authentication enabled.
2. You attempt to login to that website using your username and password.
3. If you successfully enter your password, the website will then send a code to your phone via text message. You must take that code and enter it into the website or app to successfully complete your login.
4. This code is the second factor in authentication. If you fail to enter this code correctly, you will not be able to login.

Two-factor authentication is an excellent security option for any accounts you have where you want to add an additional layer of security. Your passwords are much more likely to be stolen than access to your text messages, so two-factor authentication is a great defense against phishing attacks and password hacks. The great thing about two-factor authentication is it protects your account even if your password is stolen. A thief needs both your password and access to your text messages in order to login to your account. You may also be asked to use two-factor authentication when you try logging in to one of your accounts from a new device or location. This is just an extra security measure put in place by the website or app to protect you against fraud.

Figure 6.2 shows an example of a two-factor authentication code text message

Figure 6.2 – Example of a Two-Factor Authentication Code Text Message

Best Practice: You should use two-factor authentication if you want an additional layer of security on accounts that contain sensitive information, such as your online bank account. If you are a public figure, you should most definitely use two-factor authentication on all of your accounts, especially your social media accounts.

Order Updates

It is also common practice to receive order updates from companies you have purchased goods from online. These order updates usually include notifications of when your order has shipped and when it has been delivered. (Figure 6.3)

Figure 6.3 – Example of an Order Update Automated Text Message

Receipts

Some websites and even brick and mortar stores offer to send you receipts via text message. I do not recommend using your text messages as a way to receive receipts, as there is no easy way to store and organize them. If you are given a choice to receive a receipt by email or text, I suggest choosing the email option, and then saving those receipts in an email folder called "Receipts".

Automated Text Messages Scam

As you might have guessed, many scammers may try to fake an automated text message and fool you into giving out your sensitive information. Protecting yourself from these scams is pretty easy if you follow a couple of best practices.

Best Practice: Never reply to an automated text message with any sensitive information, including your username, password, or credit card information.

No automated text message should EVER ask you to reply with any sensitive information. A legitimate automated text message will always just provide you with the necessary information, and that's it. If an automated text message is asking you to reply with sensitive information, consider that message a scam and block the number from your phone.

Another thing to keep in mind is that a legitimate automated text message is a computer. So if for some reason you do reply to an automated text message, and it replies back to you in an intelligent and human-like fashion, then you are definitely dealing with some sort of scammer and you should block the number immediately.

Best Practice: Never click on a link inside an automated text message that is warning you about a potential security breach unless you were expecting to receive that text message.

This best practice is extremely important in protecting yourself against a potential scam. In order for a scammer to succeed, he or she needs you to provide them with sensitive information. One way for them to get that information is for you to text them back, which is already forbidden by the first best practice. The other way for them to get your information is to direct you to a fraudulent website where you would willingly disclose that information. The fraudulent website itself would be designed to look like a real website. Let's demonstrate this point with an example.

Figure 6.4.1 and 6.4.2 show two automated text messages. One of these is suspicious and the other has the potential to be legitimate. Can you tell which one is which?

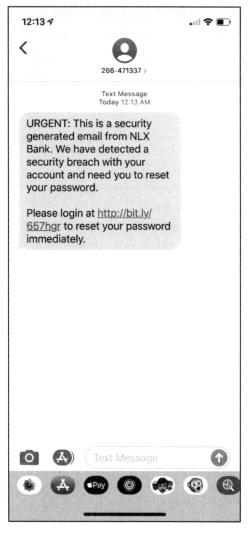

Figure 6.4.1 – Automated Security Text Message (1)

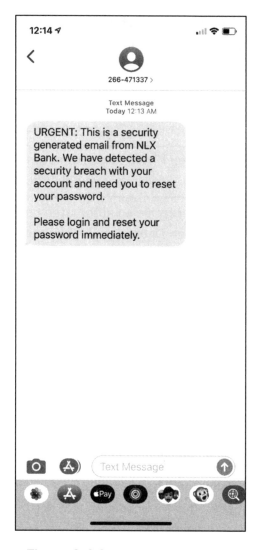

Figure 6.4.2 – Automated Security Text Message (2)

Looking at Figure 6.4.1, we see here that we are being notified that we need to reset our NLX Bank password due to a potential breach. We also see that the text message contains a link to tap on that will allow us to change our password. In Figure 6.4.2, we have nearly the same text message, except this does not provide a link and instead tells us to login to the NLX Bank website and change our password. The text message in Figure 6.4.2 is the standard industry practice in automated text messages regarding password resets, and that is that the text tells you to go to the website yourself and change your password, instead of providing a link to do so.

Think about it; which text message potentially puts you at risk? If you follow the instructions in Figure 6.4.2, there is absolutely no risk to your account information, as you will be logging in to your bank's website as you normally would. Whereas in Figure 6.4.1, you could potentially be going to a fraudulent website made to look like NLX Bank. So in this example you should treat the text message in Figure 6.4.1 as suspicious and the text message in Figure 6.4.2 as potentially legitimate.

> **Best Practice:** Treat any automated text message you receive from a regular phone number as suspicious if you did not expect to receive it.

When you receive an automated text message, they generally come from a shortened number (See Figure 6.4.2). They can however, come from a regular number as well, and this is more often seen when dealing with smaller companies, but is not completely unheard of with larger companies too. The only reason you may want to be suspicious of this automated text message is because it may be a cheap scammer who does not have the resources to afford a short code phone number.

Number Neighbors

A *Number Neighbor* is someone who has the exact same phone number as you, with the last digit being one above yours or below it. Strictly speaking, every phone number has two number neighbors. For instance, if your phone number is 555-555-5555, then your number neighbors would be 555-555-5554 and 555-555-5556. The whole concept of a number neighbor is a relatively new trend where people would randomly contact their number neighbor to say hello and chat. In fact, a number of famous cases have appeared in the media of people contacting their number neighbors and ending up becoming regular texting pals.

If you are ever contacted by your number neighbor, they will generally text message you with a greeting stating that they are your number neighbor and just want to say hello. Then a short cordial conversation generally follows where you tell each other a little about yourselves and see if you possibly share any connections, such as a mutual friend or hobby. If nothing clicks, the conversation generally ends and you will probably never hear from your number neighbor again.

The whole concept of a number neighbor may seem a little silly; the only reason is it is mentioned in this book is because it is becoming more common for some number neighbors to try and scam people. The number neighbor scam is typical of many online scams; it usually starts out with your number neighbor contacting you and trying to befriend you. Once they think they have gained your trust, they will usually ask you an unusual request. Examples of unusual requests include sending them money, signing up for their website, or agreeing to donate to one of their organizations. If you ever receive an unusual request from a number neighbor, then you should use caution and make sure you never reveal any of your sensitive information, such as your credit card details, bank details, or passwords.

Phone Call Scams & Telemarketing

Phone call scams and telemarketing have been around since the invention of the telephone and are still widely seen today with smartphones. Most people are very familiar with telemarketing calls and you have probably experienced several in your lifetime. If you find yourself overwhelmed with too many telemarketing calls on your cell phone, then you can add your phone number to the Do Not Call Registry for your country. This should stop the majority of telemarketing calls from reaching you.

Do Not Call Registry by Country

United States – www.donotcall.gov

Canada – www.lnnte-dncl.gc.ca

Australia – www.donotcall.gov.au

Adding yourself to your country's do not call list should stop the majority of telemarketing calls, however, that will not stop all of them. If you keep receiving telemarketing calls after placing yourself on the Do Not Call list, report the number that called you to your country's register.

Common Scams

Phone call scams have evolved over the years to incorporate the wide use of smartphones and technology. Protecting yourself from becoming a victim of a phone call scam can be accomplished by following a few best practices and being aware of the common types of scams.

1. *The Bank Scam*

This first scam is very common. A number you do not recognize will call you and claim to be your bank. They then will go on to tell you that your credit card or bank details may have been stolen and they need you to verify some charges. They then will go on to tell you of one or more charges that were just made on your account and ask you if you made them. After you tell them that you did not make those charges, they then tell you that they are going to cancel your card, refund the charges, and then send you a new card, *but first they need to verify your identity for security purposes*. And here is where the scam kicks in: they then will ask you for your sensitive information, such as your credit card number or social security number. What should you do?

In this situation, the phone call may be perfectly legitimate. Banks will usually try to contact you when they detect suspicious activity on your account and a phone call like this from them is fairly routine. The problem with this particular phone call is that they are asking you for sensitive information i.e. your credit card number and social security number. In order to proceed with giving out this requested information you need to first **verify** they are who they say they are. So in this situation, you should ask them a few questions. The very first question you should ask them is, if they can tell you what the three previous legitimate charges were **before** the fraudulent charges. If they can answer this accurately, then this is a positive sign, and you can proceed with the call. The next two questions you should ask them is, "Why do you need my social security number?" and "Can I use something other than my social security number to verify my identity?" If they give you suitable answers to these questions and allow you to use something other than your sensitive information, then this is a very good sign as well that the call is legitimate.

If the person you are talking to is unable to answer any of these questions accurately or satisfactorily, then you should hang up immediately, and then call the phone number on the back of your credit or debit card that was supposedly stolen and ask them about possible fraudulent charges.

> **Best Practice:** If someone contacts you claiming to be your bank and requests sensitive information, you should verify their identity by asking them to tell you about other recent transactions you have made. If you are still suspicious about the call or unsatisfied with their answers, hang up and call the phone number on the back of your credit or debit card.

> **Best Practice:** NEVER throw away paper financial statements you receive in the mail. Identity thieves try to steal these from people's trash and then use the statements against them (an identity thief who stole your thrown out bank statements may be able to answer your question about your recent transactions). Instead, you should always shred your paper statements rather than throwing them in the trash.

2. The Business Scam

The business phone call scam is very similar to the bank scam. An unknown caller who calls you will claim to be from some business you have an account with, and then proceed to tell you something is wrong with your account and they need your sensitive information to continue. This indeed could also be a completely legitimate call. For instance, if you have an automatic monthly payment with a business where you pay with your credit card, that business may call you if your credit card expires and they need to update your payment details.

You can protect yourself in this situation the same way we did with the bank example. You should ask the business a couple of questions that only the real business would know. For example, you may ask them to verify your last order with them or to tell you your account number. If you are not satisfied with the answers you receive, you should hang up and call the official phone number of the business in question.

Best Practice: You should never give out your social security number to a person over the phone who called you UNLESS you were expecting to receive that phone call. Even then, use caution when asked to disclose your sensitive information.

Mobile Phone Privacy

It is useful to know what data on your mobile phone is truly private and what is not. If privacy is very important to you, then there are steps you can take to keep your data completely private and protected from possible intrusions.

Text Messages & Messaging Privacy

Text messages on your phone are generally very secure, and can only be accessed by you, the recipients, and your cellular provider. Your text messages will remain private unless the government orders your cellular provider to turn the text messages over to them, which your provider can easily do. Some phones and apps encrypt your text messages end-to-end, which means that only you and your recipients can read them. In this scenario, both your cellular provider and the app's manufacturer cannot read them in any circumstance, and this provides the ultimate privacy. Here are some phones and apps that encrypt text messages:

Apple iPhone – If you are an Apple iPhone user, you can use what is called iMessage to send and receive text messages to other Apple device users. These messages are encrypted end-to-end and can only be read by you and the recipient. Nobody else, not even Apple can access these messages. The only way someone could access these messages was if they got access to your mobile device or if you backed up these messages to a cloud service. Please note that only messages you exchange with other Apple device users will be encrypted; regular text messages to non-Apple device users are not encrypted end-to-end and will be accessible by your cellular provider.

WhatsApp – WhatsApp is an app you can download on your smartphone that allows you to message and call other users who also have the app. WhatsApp also utilizes end-to-end encryption which means that only you and the recipient can access these messages, and WhatsApp encrypts all messages you exchange over the app.

> **Best Practice:** Using an app or service that encrypts your messages end-to-end is a very good idea for several reasons. These services basically make it impossible for anyone to hack or access your messages, unless they somehow got access to your device itself. Accordingly, you should always make sure you have security enabled on your device, which is covered next.

Securing your Mobile Device

Nearly every smartphone and tablet has the ability for you to enable some type of access security on it. Access security makes it so that only people who have the necessary credentials can access your device. An example of this security is a lock screen passcode, which is a password or PIN that must be entered each time you attempt to use your mobile device. A lock screen passcode is an excellent security option and you should absolutely have one on all of your mobile devices. If you truly want to keep the data on your mobile device secure, you should use a lock screen passcode that is at least 6 digits long and is not easily guessed.

> **Best Practice:** You should absolutely use access security on your smartphone, which will protect all of its data including your text messages from intrusion if your device were to ever fall in the wrong hands. The best access security is a lock screen passcode, and it should be at least 6 digits long and not easily guessable.

App Privacy

Apps are very popular on smartphones and tablets and there are over a million apps available for download. When downloading and using an app, you should be aware that any personal information you provide to that app will now be completely in their possession. You should also be aware that many apps collect data from you that you may not want them collecting, such as your location data. Your location data includes where you are, where you have been, and how long you have been there. There are various reasons why an app may collect this data, and it usually revolves around providing you with a better service. However, many people are uncomfortable with the notion of an app constantly tracking their location, even when they are not using the app. Fortunately, there are steps you can take to block an app from monitoring and collecting your location data.

If you want to block an app's access to your location data, you can generally do so in your smartphone or tablet's settings. You will want to look for an option such as Privacy, Location Services, or Location Tracking. Then, you should be able to enable or disable location tracking on each app you have installed on your device.

To Access Location Services on an iPhone or iPad

1. Open the Settings app
2. Tap on Privacy
3. Tap on Location Services
4. Now you can alter your location settings for your device and each app you have installed on it (Figure 6.5)

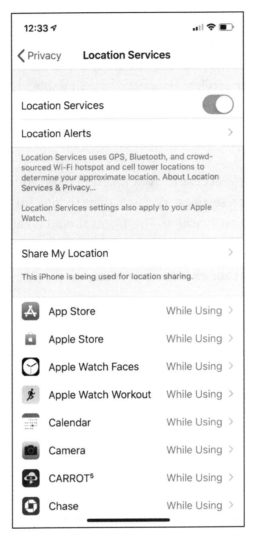

Figure 6.5 – Location Services on iPhone with iOS 13

To Access Location Services on a Samsung Galaxy Smartphone or Tablet

1. Open the Settings app
2. Tap on <u>Security</u> or <u>Biometrics and security</u>
3. Under Privacy, tap on <u>App permissions</u>
4. Tap on <u>Location</u>
5. Now you can see and alter each app that has access to your location (<u>Figure 6.6</u>)

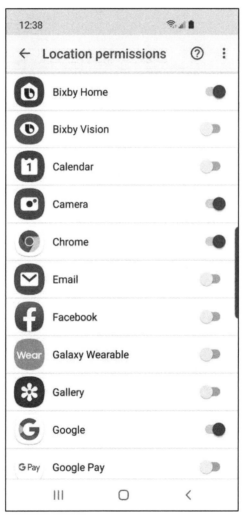

<u>Figure 6.6</u> – Location Permissions on Galaxy Smartphone Android Pie OS

Chapter 7 – Computer Safety

Being safe online while using your computer has come a long way since the early days of the internet. In the old days, you had to constantly worry about viruses, malware, and spyware infecting your computer and making it very difficult to use. Today, most computers and operating systems come with built-in protection that protect you from many types of threats, but these protections are not perfect. The fact is that your computer is likely the most vulnerable to threats out of all your devices. This is simply because computers have been around for a long time and most computers are designed to be highly customizable.

Windows PC vs. Mac vs Others

There are several types of computers out there that come in many different configurations. For the purpose of online safety, it is worth classifying computers by their operating system, and they are classified into Windows PCs, Macs, and others. A Windows PC is any computer that is running the Windows operating system. A Mac is any Apple computer that runs the Mac operating system, known as OS. The others category includes any computer that runs a different operating system other than Windows or Mac OS, such as a Chromebook or Linux computer.

Windows PCs

Windows PCs (personal computers) are by far the most common type of computers. Since they are the most common, most viruses, spyware, and malicious software are designed to infect these computers. Fortunately, Windows PCs today come with strong protection against these threats. Any computer with Windows 10, which is the newest version of the Windows operating system at the writing of this book, comes with Windows Defender, which is an antivirus and internet security application. Windows Defender is a strong basic-level protection software against some of the worst viruses and malicious attacks. In addition, Windows Defender allows you to run computer scans and remove detected malware.

Macs

A Mac is any Apple computer such as a MacBook, MacBook Pro, MacBook Air, iMac, and Mac Pro. Generally, Macs are less likely to be targeted by malicious software and this is due to several reasons. The first reason is because more people use Windows PCs than use Macs, and the law of supply and demand dictates that malicious programmers will design more software that can reach the maximum amount of people. The second reason Macs are less likely to be targeted is because of how they are designed. Macs are designed using more of a closed-system format whereas Windows PCs are more open-sourced. The pros and cons of each system are numerous, but for our purposes just know that the semi-closed system that Macs utilize provides better security against malicious software. Nonetheless, this does not mean that Mac computers are immune to threats.

Other Computers

Other computers that use an operating system other than Windows or Mac OS are just as vulnerable to attacks from malicious software. However, viruses and malicious attacks on these computers is far less likely given that they have such a smaller market share compared to PCs and Macs.

Types of Malicious Software & Nomenclature

There are many different types of malicious software and threats to your computer and they are named in various ways. To help you read this chapter, here are some definitions of the different terms used.

Malware – Malware is a general term for malicious software which is intended to harm and infect the host system. Malware is an all-encompassing term for most threats and includes viruses, spyware, adware, and ransomware.

Virus – A virus is a type of malware that is intended to infect software on your device and then spread itself. The virus itself can then do harm to your device in many different ways and can collect data from you.

Spyware – Spyware is a type of malware that is intended to monitor your activity and gather information about your system. A hacker who uses spyware then uses the data they collect from you to try and penetrate your device and get access to all of your data, including passwords and account information.

Adware – Adware is software that is meant to deliver you advertisements while you are using your device. Adware itself may not be malicious software, but it certainly can be if it is installed against your wishes and interferes with your ability to use your device.

Ransomware – Ransomware is a particularly nasty type of malware that is intended to take control of the file system in your computer and make it impossible for you to access any of your files or documents until you pay the hacker a fee. Ransomware is commonly employed against large companies who are subsequently held for ransom in order to regain access to their files.

Virus Protection Software

There is always a running debate on whether the average computer user needs third-party antivirus software, and my take is that it is better to be safe than sorry. There are many companies that offer virus protection software with many different features and perks; some name-worthy companies include Kaspersky, Norton, McAfee, and Webroot. All of these companies offer great antivirus programs that would be beneficial to use on your computer. Be that as it may, when shopping for antivirus software there are some features that you should make sure the software includes to provide you with the best protection. The features you want your antivirus software to have are:

- **Real-time Protection** – Real-time protection is essential for any antivirus software, as it protects your computer in real-time from potential attacks. If the software does not have real-time protection, then you will need to run virus scans in order to detect threats.
- **Email Security** – This is a major feature that you must have with your antivirus software. This feature will scan your emails that you receive and detect malicious attachments, potential phishing emails, and fraudulent links. The feature is not 100% foolproof, but it goes a long way in protecting you from dangerous emails.
- **Firewall** – A firewall protects your computer from hackers and network intrusions, and is essential for any antivirus software. Most computers come with a firewall, however a trusted third-party firewall is generally more robust and secure.

There are other features that an antivirus application may have that you might want to consider, such as parental controls, automatic backup of files, and safe browsing technology. These features can come in handy for certain users.

> **Best Practice:** You should purchase and use virus protection software for your computer, as it will provide you with the best possible defense against online threats. Make sure you purchase software from a well-known company and make sure it includes real-time protection, email security, and a firewall.

Many antivirus applications offer protection for your mobile devices as well. For most users, you should not need this software for your mobile devices if you have this book, although it can come in handy for email security. If you use an Apple mobile device, than you probably do not need antivirus software for your device since their operating systems are closed systems.

Keep Your Computer Up to Date

One of the best ways you can protect yourself from malware is to keep your computer up to date in every way possible. This means that whenever your computer has updates available for its operating system or system components, you should install those as soon as you can. These updates often fix vulnerabilities in the system that have been recently unearthed by hackers or malicious software. Most Windows PCs and Macs will notify you when there are updates available and direct you to update.

You should keep the applications and software you use on your computer up to date as well. These applications are often targeted by hackers, and the developers of these programs often create security updates that protect the software from known threats.

Best Practice: Nearly every computer allows you to update your computer automatically, and you should enable this to make sure your computer is always up to date.

Backing up your Data

Backing up the data on your computer is one of the most important and wise things you can do. At some point, your hard drive on your computer will fail, and you will lose all the files, documents, photos, and videos you have saved on it, unless you have everything backed up. This happens to everyone eventually and is unavoidable. Therefore, you should use an automatic backup application on your computer that automatically and continuously backs up your data to the cloud. This way, if and when you hard drive fails, all of your files will be saved on the cloud and you can easily recover them.

There are many automatic cloud backup programs you can use on your computer. Several allow you to backup a set amount of files for free and then require a monthly subscription for larger storage. My personal recommendation is a company called iDrive (www.iDrive.com). They have an excellent application and have been rated one of the best online backup service by multiple curators.

Best Practice: You should use an automatic cloud backup system on your computer if you have any important files on it, such as documents, photos, or videos. Automatic backup is a very easy and secure way to keep your files safe from hard drive crashes, and it also allows you to easily transfer your files to a new computer if you need to.

More Safety Tips for your Computer

There are a few more safety tips and best practices you can follow that will provide you with additional security against potential threats and privacy intrusions.

Cover Your Webcam when not in Use

This tip always surprises and irks people at the same time. If your computer has a webcam or you use a webcam for video chatting, then you should cover the lens of this camera whenever you are not using it. This is because hackers can potentially activate your camera remotely and spy on you using your webcam! These hackers can also make it so you have no idea you are being recorded by making sure the record light does not illuminate while it is recording. This creepy practice has been known to happen, so protect yourself by covering your webcam with a piece of opaque tape or another object whenever you are not using it. Some antivirus programs also offer webcam protection, however I still recommend you cover the camera whenever it is not in use.

Clean out your Computer Annually

Once a year, you should go through your computer and uninstall any programs you never use or plan to never use in the future. You should also look for programs that are installed that you have never heard of and look suspicious. This is a good practice to follow as it keeps your computer running smoothly and saves you hard drive space. You should also take caution not to uninstall any programs that your computer needs to function properly. If you are unsure whether you should uninstall something or not, simply perform a web search of "Should I uninstall *program/app name*?" To properly uninstall something, use the Remove Apps feature in the Control Center of your Windows PC. For Macs, you can simply delete an app from your Applications folder.

Run a Full-System Scan Periodically

If you have antivirus software installed on your computer, you should run a full system scan once every 3 months or whenever you suspect something is wrong with your computer. A full system scan can uncover and remove potentially dangerous threats that your real-time protection was not able to detect.

Use Caution when Installing Software you have downloaded from the Internet

When downloading and installing software from the internet, there are a couple of things you want to look out for. If you use antivirus software, then this software will usually detect and notify you if the software you downloaded is troublesome, and you can stop right there. However, it will not detect some sneaky installation options that you have to choose when installing the software. An example of this is when installing one program, the installation software asks you if you want to install an additional program that you most likely do not want. This is a somewhat common practice when installing freeware (software that is free to download and use). These additional applications are generally annoying and could potentially be adware. Make sure when you are installing any software that you pay close attention to the prompts that appear on your screen, and you only check off the applications you want installed and uncheck any software that you have no interest in. Watch out for browser toolbar installations and requests to change your default search engine or home page.

Install a Third-party Video Player on your Computer

Your computer most likely comes with a pre-installed video player that can play most video types. Despite this, the pre-installed video players are not the best, and you will often encounter problems when trying to use them for certain videos. I recommend you download a trusted third-party video software that will play all videos and not interfere with your device. My personal recommendation is the VLC media play (www.videolan.org) that is free to download and use, and is immensely popular with its users.

Recommended Software and Apps

In this section I will provide you with a list of recommended software and apps for your PC or Mac. Not all of these applications have to do with online safety, but they all are trusted applications with a proven track record of safety and reliability. They also can come in handy for common uses on computers.

Recommended Windows PC Software and Apps

- Microsoft Office / Office 365 (Word, Excel, Outlook, & PowerPoint) – Available at www.microsoft.com
- Adobe Acrobat – PDF Viewer available at www.adobe.com
- VLC Video Plater – Video player available at www.videolan.org

Recommended Mac Applications

- Office 365 – Microsoft Office for the Mac, available in the App Store (Alternatively, you can download Pages, Keynote, and Numbers)
- VLC Video Player – Video player available at www.videolan.org

Chapter 8 – Online Dating Safety

In this chapter, we will cover the many aspects of safety when using online dating websites and apps. If you do not use any online dating services, do not plan to use online dating, or do not have children who may use online dating, then you can skip this chapter entirely.

Online Dating Platforms

Online dating has become immensely popular in recent years and can be a great way to meet someone. There are many different online dating platforms available, and they each have their own unique features, reputation, and demographic usage. Most of these platforms are available both on the web and through an app, and some are free to use while others charge a subscription fee. In my humble opinion, online dating platforms that charge a monthly fee to all of its users tend to have people who are looking for more serious relationships than just casual flings.

Match.com – Match.com was one of the first online dating platforms and still remains one of the most popular platforms today. Match.com charges a monthly fee to become a user, and their users are diverse in terms of age, income, hobbies, and personalities. Furthermore, Match.com has a reputation and history for matchmaking serious relationships and companionship. Like most online dating websites, Match.com operates by you creating a profile for yourself and filling in some information, such as your interests, hobbies, location, and what kind of relationship you are looking for. Then you can fill in information about your ideal match, and Match.com will attempt to show you other profiles that you may find suitable. If any of these profiles interest you, you can send them a message and see where it goes. Other platforms similar to Match.com include eHarmony and Chemistry.com.

Tinder – Tinder is an app-based online dating platform that is free to use and is famous for its swipe right and swipe left matching system. The way it works is first you can download and use the app on your smartphone for free. Once you have downloaded the app, you then create your profile using basic information and a photo or two. The photo you choose is extremely important as that is how you will be quickly judged by other users. Once your profile is set, you can begin looking for matches. Tinder will show you profile pictures of users who are near your location, and you can swipe right to approve a profile or swipe left to disapprove. If a profile you approved also swipes right on your profile, then you will be a match and be allowed to message each other. If you both do not approve each other, then you will be unable to message. Tinder is popular in the age group of people under 35, although people in a higher age bracket can be found on there as well. Furthermore, it is common for people to be seeking casual relationships on Tinder. Other platforms similar to Tinder include Bumble and Hinge.

OKCupid & Plenty of Fish – OKCupid and Plenty of Fish are two separate online dating platforms. Both platforms are free to join, and both have apps along with websites you can use. Their systems and matchmaking work similar to other dating websites, and their user base is very diverse in terms of age, although it leans more towards the younger side. Both of these platforms are also diverse in terms of what users are looking for. Many people are looking for serious relationships while many others are looking for something casual or just to chat.

Specialty Platforms – Other online dating platforms exist that focus on a certain defining characteristic that all of its users share. For example, Christian Mingle is an online dating platform for Christian singles whereas JDate is an online dating platform for Jewish singles. Black People Meet is an online dating platform exclusively for black singles. There are many other platforms that are tailored around other characteristics as well.

Protecting Yourself

When using online dating platforms, you should protect yourself from scammers and predators who may also be using the platform. Ordinarily, you may find that there are more scammers using the free online dating platforms compared to the ones that charge a fee. In addition, there are a number of fake profiles on free dating platforms that you may encounter, and recognizing a fake profile is imperative in the effort to protect yourself from being scammed and wasting your time. In this section we will cover the best practices to follow that will protect you while online dating.

Best Practice: Never Disclose your Exact Location in your Profile

This should be common sense, but you should never give away your exact location in your profile. This includes any pictures that may give away your address, such as a photo that shows your house address in the background. Likewise, you should never disclose your full name in your profile unless the platform you are using requires it. These are just preventative measures you can apply to prevent predators from knowing exactly who you are and where you live without ever having talked to you.

Best Practice: Never Take another User's Profile at Face Value

People on online dating platforms lie or embellish all the time, especially in their profile. A certain amount of this is to be expected, as people want to put the best information about themselves and their best photos front and center on their profile, even if they are from 10 years ago. So keep in mind that when viewing anyone's profile that the information they provided might be exaggerated or downright false, including their age, location, occupation, or anything else that appears. Another common practice found on online dating platforms is the embellishment of profile photos. This is done in a number of ways, from adding filters to a photo to hide blemishes or make them look younger, or using an older photo that is completely out of date. This practice is not necessarily a huge risk to your safety, but is important that you are aware of it.

Best Practice: Never go to a Verification Website that another User Directs you to

This is a common scam that fake profiles use on their victims. The way it works is you begin messaging with a match you have on an online dating platform, and everything seems too good to be true. This person you are messaging with wants to meet, but is concerned about safety so they ask you to verify your identity and background at a website link that they have provided to you. This link would take you off the online dating platform that you are using and they say the website will verify that you are not a criminal, that you do not have a violent history, and that you are who you say you are. This is a complete scam as presumably the website you are directed to will charge you for this service, and the person who you are chatting with will have no desire to meet after they have collected that payment, or worse, stolen your credit card details through the fraudulent website. Therefore, if someone you are messaging with on a dating platform asks you to verify your identity through an outside website, then you are probably chatting with a fraudulent profile and should cease contact with them immediately and report them to the platform.

Best Practice: Beware of Pay-to-Play Scams

When using free online dating platforms, you are bound to come across this type of user as well. A pay-to-play scheme is when a user directs you to pay them in order for them to keep talking to you or to gain access to all of their content. This scam is very similar to the premium Snapchat scheme covered in Chapter 5 of this book. These users are most likely violating the terms of service of the dating platform, and are just on the platform to make money. So if anyone ever asks you for money in order for them to keep talking with you, you should know that this person is most likely just trying to cash in and is not interested in dating per se.

Investigating and Verifying Other Users

When you are messaging users on an online dating platform, you already know to watch out for scams, predators, and fake profiles. In this section I will show you how you can determine if a profile is suspicious and likely to be fake. None of these practices are 100% dependable, however they will help you make a better decision on whether a profile is legitimate or not.

Take Note on How Many Photos they have on their Profile

The first red flag that indicates a profile may be suspicious is if they only have one photo of themselves. This is suspicious because the average person has more than one photo of themselves in their possession, and a person trying to create a fake profile to scam someone is more likely to only use one photo. Now it is certainly possible that the profile that only has one photo is perfectly legitimate, but it would be prudent of you to ask this person during your communications if they could send you another photo of themselves to help you verify they are real.

You should also take note of the types of photos they have posted on their profile. If every single photo is professionally done, then that may indicate that the profile could be suspicious (they may be using the photos of a professional model or actor). If every photo partially blocks their face (sunglasses, blurry, zoomed out, etc.), then that is another red flag that may make a profile suspicious.

Do a Web Search and Social Media Search on the Person's Name

If the person you are chatting with has given you their full name, you may want to run your own quick online background check of the person if you plan to meet them. Some people say this may spoil the surprise of meeting them, but with online dating, safety should be one of your primary concerns. You can do a web search of the person's name to see if anything interesting comes up, such as a LinkedIn profile which will tell you their occupation. You can also do a social media search on Facebook or Twitter to see if you can view more information about them. This can be especially helpful if you want to verify the age of the person you are chatting with.

If you think a Profile is Suspicious, ask them Questions about your Local Neighborhood

Most online dating platforms use your location to find you matches, so chances are you may be talking with someone from a neighboring town or city. If you think a person you are messaging with is potentially a fake profile; a good test to perform is to ask them questions about the area that only locals would know.

Meeting someone you met Online

When using an online dating platform, you may eventually reach the point where you really connect with a user and agree to meet. It is important to recognize that online dating begins with a high level of anonymity, and is not the same as dating someone you know through mutual friends. Therefore, you should take some common sense precautions when agreeing to meet with someone you encounter online.

- Meet in a public place, and tell a friend where you are going, who you are meeting with, and when you are meeting.
- Use separate transportation to meet. Do not have an internet stranger pick you up from your place or theirs.
- Have a backup plan in case you really do not like the person and become uncomfortable and want to leave.

Chapter 9 – Online Safety for Parents with Children

Online safety for children is a major concern for parents as the internet without limits can be an especially dangerous place. Parents often worry that their children will do something irresponsible or end up being victimized by a scammer or predator. Fortunately, you have this book to help prepare you to keep your children safe while using the internet, and this book focuses on two principles to accomplish this: education and prevention. Education is the most important tool when it comes to protecting your kids from online threats. You need to be educated on what is happening on the internet and your child needs to be educated on online safety as well. The majority of this chapter focuses on online safety for parents with teenagers, as they use the internet considerably and are more at risk. For parents with younger children, the parental controls section will be especially helpful to you, as well as the unauthorized purchases section at the end of the chapter.

Education: The First Step is the #1 Rule of Social Media

The very first thing you should do when it comes to educating your children about using the internet and social media safely is to hammer home the #1 Rule of Social Media, which is **There is no such thing as privacy when using social media, and anything you share on social media will <u>forever</u> be public**. If you can educate your children about the importance of this rule, the rest will be easy. Both you and your children need to understand what this rule means, and its implications.

The first part of the rule states that there is no such thing as privacy when using social media. This means that everything you post or share on any social media platform is available for everyone to see and can always be linked back to you. The second part is even more ominous, and that is that anything you post, say, or share on social media will forever be public and cannot be permanently deleted. This means that absolutely anything you share on social media will be available for anyone in the public to see 10, 20, 30, or even 40 years in the future. It may seem ridiculous that something you post on social media when you were 14 can prevent you from getting a job when you are 30, but sadly it happens all the time (just perform a web search for "fired for past tweets" and see what I mean). In the real world, you can have most things from your childhood erased from the public record including your academic behavior, driving record, and even your arrest record, but you cannot have your social media history completely erased because the internet never forgets, and it will never let you forget either.

This #1 Rule is the guiding principle for educating children on how to use the internet and social media safely. Social media and the internet itself are deeply intertwined, so there is little difference between the two in today's age when it comes to online safety. Social media can be defined as any online platform (app or website) that allows you to communicate with others, and includes posting platforms, forums, chat and messaging apps, photo and video sharing apps, comment boards, and even apps that allow you to post anonymously.

Education: Know what your Children are using

This is a notoriously difficult task for any parent, and that is finding out what your child is using on the internet. They could be using any number of social media platforms, apps, and devices. Even more difficult is keeping up with the changing trends of young people. One month it may be one app that every teenager is using and the next month it may be something else. Fortunately, there are many resources on the internet to help you keep up with the changing trends. One such resource is www.infinityguides.com, which has news and online courses for new technology, social media, and apps. Of course the best way to find out what technology your children are using is to talk with them and ask them about it. Alternatively, you can use parental controls to see what your children are doing online, which we will cover shortly.

As of the time of this book's writing, there are several platforms that teenagers use regularly:

- **Instagram** – Social media app very popular among teenagers.
- **Snapchat** – Picture and video sharing app very popular among teenagers.
- **Twitter** – Social media app and website popular with teens and celebrities.
- **Pinterest** – Posting board social media app and website popular with adolescent women.
- **Facebook** – Not as popular with teens and young adults as it used to be, but most teenagers maintain a presence on it.
- **TikTok** – Chinese video sharing app whose popularity is trending upwards with teenagers and young adults.
- **Tumblr** – A message board social media platform that is not as popular as it once was, but some teens use it to follow their favorite celebrities and interact with friends.

Education: Social Media Risks

Each social media platform has its own risks for children and teenagers. As a parent, it is important for you to be educated on these risks so you know what your children may be exposed to. Before embarking on this section, I recommend you read Chapter 5 on social media safety to get a full understanding of the different platforms.

Facebook

Facebook is the most popular social media platform and it is also one of the safest for your child to use. Teenagers and children typically use Facebook to exchange messages with friends, plan parties and events, and collaborate on projects for school. In addition, it is very common for events to be organized on Facebook, whether it be a party, social event, or get-together. The biggest risk a child can encounter on Facebook is an interaction with a stranger. A stranger may send a friend request to your child, and then start messaging them for any reason whatsoever. Many parents teach their children not to interact with strangers on the street; the same lesson could be prudent for strangers on the internet as well.

The next risk your child may experience on Facebook is bullying. If your child is bullied at school, there is a good chance they are bullied on social media as well, and it can be on any platform. Keep a sharp eye out for bullying content on your child's Facebook profile and take appropriate action if you encounter it. Social media bullying is a serious problem among school-aged children and can have serious consequences as the bullying can be constant.

Instagram

Instagram is a very popular social media platform with teenagers and is most commonly used through its smartphone app. The way Instagram works is people post pictures, usually of themselves, with captions and their followers like and comment on the pictures. Their followers can be friends, acquaintances, or even random people. The risk comes from strangers who may try to interact with your child on the platform. Some of the most popular accounts on Instagram are attractive women who post beautiful photos of themselves. They attract thousands upon thousands of followers and many then attempt to monetize their account by promoting products. Unfortunately, there are some dreadful people on Instagram who try and digitally stalk people online, and may even contact them through a direct message. This is where you child can potentially become at risk.

If you allow your child to have an Instagram account, you should also create an Instagram account for yourself and follow your child (Figure 9.1). That way you can see exactly what they post to their account, and you can see the comments that other people put on the post (Figure 9.2). You should also be aware that your teenager may create a secondary account, in which they post photos and videos that they do not want their regular followers (such as their parents and family members) to see.

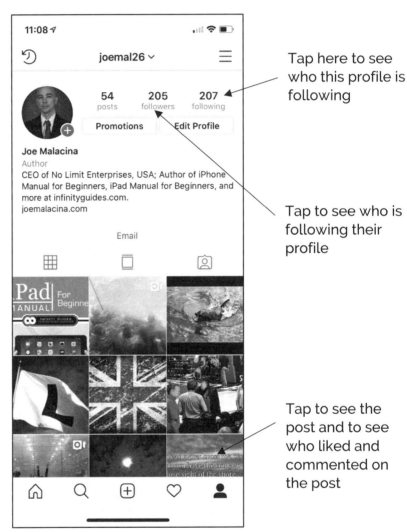

Tap here to see who this profile is following

Tap to see who is following their profile

Tap to see the post and to see who liked and commented on the post

Figure 9.1 – Viewing Someone's Profile on Instagram

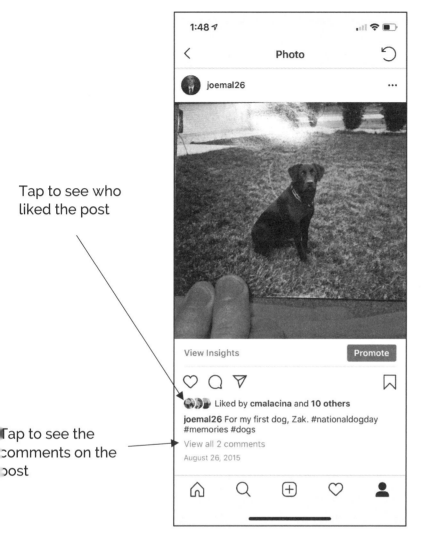

Tap to see who
liked the post

Tap to see the
comments on the
post

Figure 9.2 – Viewing a Post on Instagram

Snapchat

Snapchat is another social media app that is extremely popular with teenagers. The app works by allowing users to send and receive disappearing photos and videos to each other. The whole allure of the app is that the photos and videos people send to each other disappear, so they cannot be saved and potentially shared with others. But you know better, you know the #1 Rule of Social Media, and you know that nothing you share on social media is private, and is in fact forever public. This holds true with

Snapchat as well, and if you need a refresher as to why that is, please see the Snapchat section of Chapter 5.

It is very important for your teenager to know the #1 Rule of Social Media applies to Snapchat. That way, they will not make the same mistake that many teenagers have in thinking whatever they send over the app will remain private. There have been numerous documented cases of teenagers using the Snapchat app to "sext" each other, and later finding out those private images they sent have been shared and circulated among fellow classmates. Sexting (sext) means to send sexual text, images, or videos to another person with a smartphone, tablet, or computer. Not only is sexting humiliating if it becomes public, it also illegal in many countries including the United States to send sexual pictures of yourself to another person if you are legally underage. Your teenager, if underage, could potentially be charged and prosecuted for distributing child pornography if they were to send a sexual image or video of themselves to someone.

Twitter

Twitter is another popular social media platform among teenagers, and it carries certain risks worth noting. The first risk is the fact that strangers can easily contact your child on Twitter and strike up a conversation. The conversation could be very vanilla or more predatory. The second risk is online bullying. There is plenty of bullying, shaming, and ostracizing going around on Twitter and that is to be expected on the platform especially if you delve into politics. What you need to watch out for with your child is explicit bullying from his or her classmates, as this could mean they are also being bullied at school. One of the big problems of social media is if your child is bullied at school, they then come home and have to deal with bullying online. In other words, there is no escape and the torment never ends. So if you suspect your child is bullied at school, keep a close eye on their social media accounts to see if it continues on there.

The last risk of Twitter for children is the potential exposure to pornography. Pornography is allowed on Twitter, however if you are not seeking it out then it is unlikely that it will ever appear on your feed. Unfortunately, sometimes a Twitter user can stumble upon the pornography, and then they may become inundated with it. Furthermore, if they are seeking pornography on Twitter, it is all too easy to find.

Other Social Media Platforms

For all other social media platforms and apps, the risks your child faces is generally the same, with the biggest risk being the potential contact with strangers who wish to victimize or take advantage of your child. As long as you and your teenager know and understand the #1 Rule of Social Media, then you are more than halfway through the battle of keeping your child safe online.

Education: Other Online Risks for Children

For the most part, the biggest online risk for children comes from their use of social media websites and apps. The other risks that they are susceptible to are the same risks that you are vulnerable against, such as email attacks, viruses and malware, online shopping scams, and smartphone related scams. You can protect them from the majority of these threats by educating them about these dangers and taking basic prevention steps to stop them from occurring in the first place, such as installing antivirus software on your teenager's computer. Luckily, many teenagers and young adults are very adept at recognizing and stopping online scams and phishing attempts, even more so than many adults. So the amount of education they may need on that subject could be very relatively small.

Prevention: Parental Controls

The second principle of online safety for parents with children is prevention. Prevention is proactively taking the necessary steps to protect your children from the various threats of using the internet and social media. The first part of prevention is parental controls. Parental controls are tools for parents that allow you to control what your child can and cannot do on his or her device. Parental controls are not a perfect solution in any sense, and they cannot prevent your child from accessing everything. They can however provide significant safeguards that allow you to control and monitor your child's online activity.

Before we explore what you can do with parental controls, a couple of caveats about these systems are worth noting. First, you must understand that no parental control system is perfect, and that there is always a way for your child to get around the parental controls if they are really determined and clever. This is just a fact of technology and there is no way around it. Secondly, parental control systems vary greatly depending upon how you want to use them. For instance, there are parental controls you can set up on your computer, there are parental controls you can set up on your child's mobile device, and finally there are third-party parental controls you can set up for social media. All of these different types of parental controls can make things a little complicated, so I will do my best to provide you with the easiest solutions.

Computer Level Parental Controls

The first type of parental control you should enable are the computer level parental controls, and these are the easiest to set up. Computer level parental controls allow you to control how your children can use the computer and can easily be setup on a Windows PC or Mac Computer.

Windows PC Parental Controls

To setup parental controls on a Windows PC (Windows 10), follow these steps.

1. Click the start icon and then click on the settings icon. (Figure 9.3)

Figure 9.3 – Accessing Windows Settings from Start Menu

2. Click on Accounts in Windows Settings.
3. Click on family & other users.
4. The first thing you want to do is create family member accounts for your children. I recommend creating a separate account for each child that you allow to use the computer. Click on Add a family member.

5. When you create a family member user, you will need to create a Microsoft account for them. Go ahead and do so and follow the instructions on your screen.

Once you have successfully created a family member account for your child, you then can create restrictions and other controls for your child's account. Windows PCs have a great parental control system, and there is much you can customize:

- **Activity Reports** – Activity reports allow you to get email reports on your child's activity on their computer usage including their website history, apps they are using, and how much time they are spending on each.
- **Schedule screen time** – With Windows Family Controls, you can schedule certain hours of the day that your child is allowed to use the computer. If they attempt to use the computer outside of the scheduled screen time, they will not be allowed to do so.
- **Content Filters** – You can also set content filters for your child's account, which allows you to set certain restrictions on the type of content they can access. You may want to restrict their ability to purchase things from the Microsoft Store. You can also set a content filter to block inappropriate apps, games, and media. Lastly, you can block your child from accessing inappropriate websites so long as they are using the Microsoft Edge internet browser.
- **Location Tracking** – If your child has a laptop and you set up their family member account on it, then at any time you can track your child's location and location history.

For a full list and walkthrough of how to use a Windows PC Family Controls, visit https://support.microsoft.com/en-us/help/12413/microsoft-account-what-is-family-group

Mac Computer Parental Controls

To setup parental controls on a Mac computer or any Apple device, follow these steps (Steps indicated are specific for a Mac computer):

1. The first thing you need to do is set up a family account with your Apple ID, and create a family user for your child. To do this, follow steps 2-5.
2. Open System Preferences from your Dock or Launchpad.
3. Click on Family Sharing, and then click on the plus sign to create a new user. (Figure 9.4)

Figure 9.4 – Accessing Family Sharing from System Preferences (Mac)

4. Click on <u>Create an Apple ID for a child who doesn't have an account</u>.
5. Fill in the requested information on the next screen. You will need to create an Apple ID email address for your child.
6. Next, you need to create a user account on your Mac for your child, which you can do from <u>Users & Groups</u> option in System Preferences.
7. Now click on the <u>plus sign</u> to create a user account for your child. Fill in the requested information and create a password if you'd like for your child to access the Mac. (You may need to click on the lock icon before you can click on the plus sign.) (<u>Figure 9.5</u>)

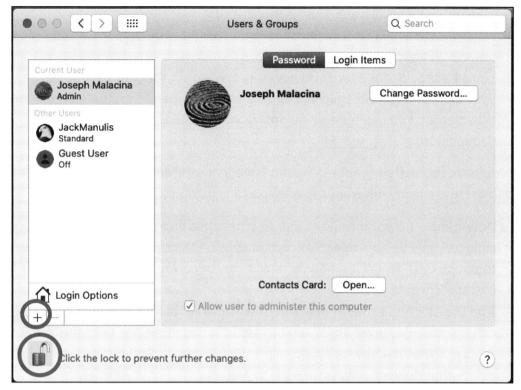

Figure 9.5 – Creating a new user for your child on a Mac

8. Once the account has been created, you will need to log out of your account on the Mac, and log in with the child's account. This can be down use the Apple icon at the top of your Mac's screen.

9. The first time you log in to the Mac with your child's account, you will be asked to sign in with your child's Apple ID and password that you created earlier. Go ahead and do so.

10. Once you have logged in, your Mac will set up the account on your computer. Continue following the instructions on your screen until you are brought to your desktop.

11. Now go ahead and log out of your child's account, and log back in to your account on the Mac

12. Now open System Preferences and click on Family Sharing.

13. On the left, click on Screen Time.

14. Now on the left, click on the drop down box and select your child's account. (See Figure 9.6)

15. At the bottom left of the Screen Time window, click on Options. (See Figure 9.6)

16. Click on <u>Turn On</u> if Screen Time is listed as off.
17. Now you can set various parental controls to limit your child's use and see reports on your child's activity.
18. You also should make sure you have a password set for your user account on your Mac, or else your child will be able to access it and have unlimited access to the internet. You can set a password for your main account in the Users & Groups setting. (<u>Figure 9.5</u>)

Once you have successfully enabled Screen Time (parental controls) on your child's account, there are many different aspects you can customize:

- **Downtime** – Downtime allows you to schedule a downtime session where your child will only be able to access certain apps on their phone and only have access to phone calls. You can schedule downtime for certain hours every day or set a custom schedule.
- **App Limits** – App Limits allows you to set time limits for app usage based on categories and specific apps. You can set up a daily time limit or a custom limit.
- **Always Allowed** – Always Allowed lets you choose which apps on your child's device that they are always allowed to use.
- **Content & Privacy** – Content & Privacy allows you to restrict certain content on your child's device or account.
    - ○ **Content** – Choose which type of web and game content you want your child to have access to. (<u>Figure 9.6</u>)

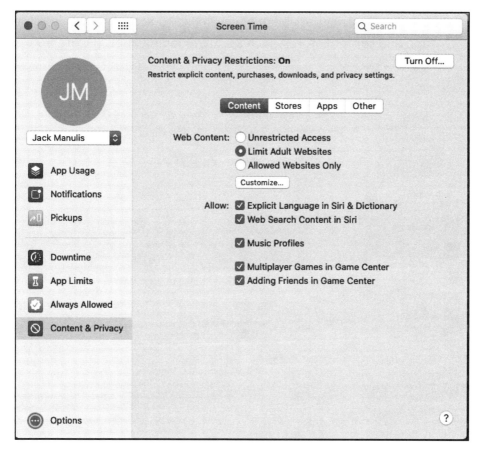

Figure 9.6 – Screen Time: Setting Content Restrictions

o **Stores** – Restrict the ability of your child to access certain items in Apple's app and content stores, such as downloading apps. (Figure 9.7)

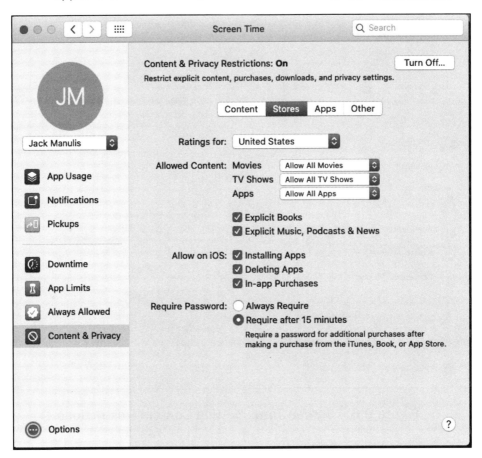

Figure 9.7 – Screen Time: Setting Store Restrictions

○ **Apps –** Decide which apps your child is allowed to use and which ones they are not allowed to use. (<u>Figure 9.8</u>)

<u>Figure 9.8</u> – Screen Time: Setting App Restrictions

- Other – Allows you to restrict certain changes on the child's iPhone or iPad, such as passcode changes. (Figure 9.9)

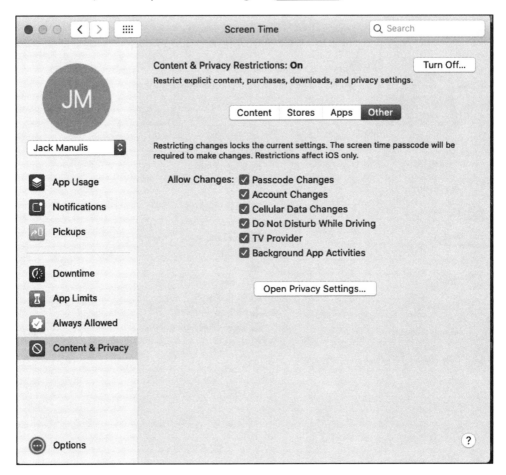

Figure 9.9 – Screen Time: Setting Other Restrictions

- **Options –** Options in Screen Time allow you to alter a couple of settings. I recommend you set up a Screen Time passcode to prevent your parental control settings from being changed.

Once you have set up a child account and configured Screen Time settings for that child, those settings will apply to all of the devices your child has an account on, including any Mac, iPhone, or iPad.

Mobile Device Level Parental Controls

You can also setup parental controls on most smartphones and tablets that your child uses.

Apple iPhone or iPad Parental Controls

Setting up parental controls on an iPhone or iPad for your child is very simple. The first thing you need to do is make sure you have created a separate Apple ID for your child, and that they are not using the same Apple ID as you. Then, you need to add that Apple ID to your family. To do this, follow these steps (If you already set up a child account on your Mac, then you are already good to go and you just need to make sure your child's mobile device is signed in with their family member account [see step 6].):

1. On **your** iPhone or iPad, open the Settings app and tap on your name at the top. If you do not have an iPhone or iPad, you can use your Mac computer instead, in which case follow the *Mac Computer Parental Controls*)
2. Tap on Family Sharing.
3. Tap Add Family Member...
4. Tap Create a Child Account.
5. Follow the instructions on your screen to create an Apple ID for your child. Once this step is complete, move on to step 6.
6. Ideally, you will have not set up your **child's iPhone or iPad** at all yet. If this is the case for you, power the device on and follow the instructions on your screen. When you come to the Apple ID screen, choose that you already have an Apple ID, and login with your child's Apple ID.
    a. If you have already set up your child's iPhone or iPad, then you can reset the device to factory settings. This will delete all of the data on the device, including apps, contacts, photos, and videos and start the device from scratch. To reset the device, open Settings -> General -> Reset -> Erase all Content and Settings.
    b. If you do not want to completely erase the device, there is a workaround. You can try to invite the Apple ID that your child is using on their device to your family and then accept the invitation through your child's device or Apple ID email. You also need to make sure your child is signed with their Apple ID on their mobile device.
7. Once your child's iPhone or iPad is set up using the Apple ID you created for them, there is nothing left for you to do on your child's device.

8. Now on **your iPhone or iPad**, open Settings and tap on Screen Time.
9. Scroll down and look for your family. Tap on the name of your child's account.
10. Now you will be able to set various parental controls for your child's account and devices. For a full description of what controls you can customize, see the *Mac Computer Parental Controls* section earlier in this chapter. (Figure 9.10)

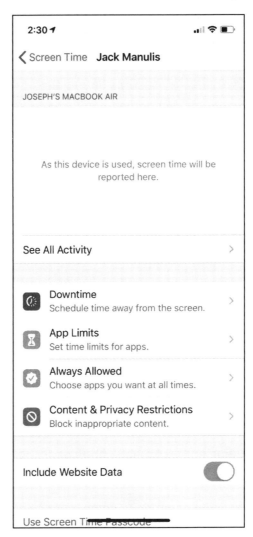

Figure 9.10 – Setting Parental Controls using Screen Time on an iPhone or iPad

Android Phone or Tablet Parental Controls

Parental controls on an Android device are natively limited compared to Apple devices. With the native parental controls, you can limit what apps your child is allowed to download, and which content they are allow to see on the Play Store, such as movies, music, television, and books. There are two different ways you can set up these Play Store parental controls on an Android mobile device. The first way is to take your child's device, and manually set the parental controls. This way is the easiest to perform, and can be accomplished by performing these steps:

1. On your **child's device**, open the <u>Play Store app</u>.
2. Tap on the <u>menu icon (three horizontal lines)</u>, then tap <u>Settings</u>, then tap <u>Parental Controls</u>
3. Tap the <u>enable icon</u> at the top to enable Parental Controls and create a PIN.
4. Once your PIN is set, you can set which type of content your child is allowed to download from the Play Store. (<u>Figure 9.11</u>)

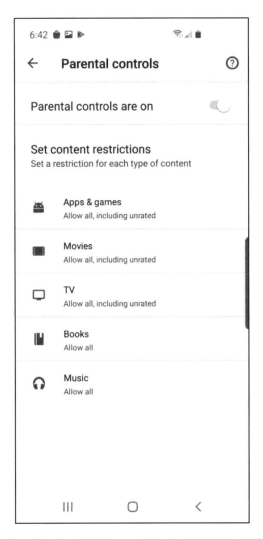

Figure 9.11 – Setting Parental Controls on an Android Device
(Play Store -> Menu -> Settings -> Parental Controls)

The second way to enable parental controls is through the Family Link app, which allows you to add a child user account to your family, and then set up the same exact parental controls.

In additional, there are several third party apps you can use for parental controls for an Android device, and many antivirus software companies offer these (covered in chapter 7). These third party providers are excellent for more customized parental control systems.

Software and Platform Level Parental Controls

Software and platform level parental controls are rare when it comes to the platform itself having a native parental controls system. You would be hard pressed to find any type of parental controls when looking through a social media platform's settings. Your computer level parental controls, as well as Apple's Screen Time are adequate for restricting access to certain apps, websites, and content, however, if you want a more advanced parental control system that has more monitoring and blocking controls, you will have to use a third-party system. Here are a couple of my recommended third-party parental control applications. You can find these by doing a web search for their name.

- Qustodio
- WebWatcher
- FamilyTime
- Net Nanny

Prevention: Financial Data for your Child

Children making unauthorized purchases online is a common situation encountered by many parents who end up stuck with the bill. Fortunately, there are several things you can do to prevent this type of situation from occurring.

Create an Email Address for your Child

If you plan on allowing your child to use mobile devices or have a computer, then you should definitely create an email address for them that you also have access to. This is important as it allows you to separate your account from theirs while still allowing you to maintain full control over their account. Then, when your child gets their own mobile device they can log in with the email address you created for them (nearly every mobile device requires that you create or log in to an account with an email address). Your credit card will not necessarily be linked to their account so you do not have to worry about any unauthorized purchases.

Make Use of Prepaid Debit Cards

A prepaid debit card is a great way to manage a digital allowance for your child. You can put a set amount on the card at regular intervals, and you will never have to worry about your child spending more than what you allotted. You can even manage the account and review your child's purchases online.

Prevention: Built-in Tools

You already have several built-in tools at your disposable for protecting your child's safety online. We have already covered how your Windows PC, Mac, tablet, and smartphone all have built-in parental controls that you can utilize. Furthermore, many other devices, apps, and services have built-in parental controls that you can employ for additional security. For instance, if your family uses the Netflix streaming service then you have some controls that you can customize for your child, such as limiting what shows or movies they can watch, removing titles with an inappropriate rating, and creating separate profiles for different people in your family.

For every internet-ready device and service that your child uses, you should check to see if it has any built-in parental controls. Some common devices and apps that have parental controls include:

- Smart TVs
- Cable TV boxes
- YouTube and YouTube for Kids
- Amazon devices
- Smart Thermostats

Best Practices

In this final section, we will summarize most of the content in this chapter through some best practices. There are also a few best practices that were not covered that are worth noting.

Best Practice: Know and understand the #1 Rule of Social Media, and make sure your children also know and understand it. This #1 Rule provides the basis for all of social media safety and much of internet safety.

If you need a reminder, the #1 Rule of Social Media is: **There is no such thing as privacy when using social media, and anything you share on social media will <u>forever</u> be public**.

Best Practice: Education and prevention are the two main principles of keeping your children safe while using the internet. Education involves educating yourself and your children on the various risks of online safety, and prevention involves taking active steps to prevent your children from harmful content and online activity.

Best Practice: Start making use of parental controls right away!

The sooner you start using parental controls, the easier it will be to manage your child's online activity. If you start parental controls late, then your child may have already been exposed to harmful content and the avenue in which they were exposed may still be available to them after parental controls have been implemented.

Best Practice: Keep up with the online trends of young people, as they are often changing.

This is a hard best practice to follow, as the online trends of young people change so frequently. Fortunately, some of those trends last a very long time, such as young people's preferred use of Snapchat and Instagram for social media. Here is a more complete list of apps and social media platforms teenagers are using:

- Snapchat (photo sharing)
- Instagram (photo sharing)
- Pinterest (posting board, popular with adolescent girls)
- Tellonym (anonymous messaging app)
- Kik (messaging app, very popular with American teens)
- Holla (video chatting app with strangers)
- Houseparty (video chatting app)
- Telegram (messaging app with secret messages)

If you want to see exactly what these apps do and what type of content they have, I recommend you download them to your device and check them out.

Best Practice: Know the different risks children are often exposed to online. Teenagers are often targeted by online predators and scammers, whereas with young children you want to make sure they do not stumble across harmful content.

The majority of this chapter is focused on how to keep your teenager safe while using the internet, simply because many teenagers use the internet regularly. You should also be aware that teenagers are very clever, and have many tools at their disposable to hide their online activity. In fact, there are some apps available that were created to assist in this purpose. One such example was a private messaging app, whose app icon appeared to look like a calculator so outsiders or parents would never think of opening it on their child's device. If you want to have better control over your child's online activity, then I highly suggest implementing parental controls early.

141

Acronyms Commonly Used by Teens

Acronyms are very commonly used when communicating online, especially by teenagers. You should know what the most common acronyms are and what they mean so you can interpret a conversation when you read it. Teenagers are notorious for filling their messages with as many acronyms as possible, and some of these can be worrisome if you come across them. In the appendix of this text is a large list of acronyms commonly used on the internet, and it would be wise to familiarize yourself with them. Listed below are some acronyms that are known to be used by some teenagers that you definitely want to be able to recognize if encountered:

- CD9 – Code 9, parents around (meant to notify someone that they cannot message freely as their parents are around)
- GNOC – Get naked on camera
- KMS – Kill myself (usually used in a sarcastic manner)
- LH6 – Let's have sex
- LMIRL – Let's meet in real life
- MOS – Mom over shoulder (meant to notify someone that they cannot message freely as their parents are around)
- POS – Parent(s) over shoulder (can sometimes mean 'piece of excrement')
- PAH – Parents are home
- PAL – Parents are listening (meant to notify someone that they cannot message freely as their parents are around)

Chapter 10 – What to do when you're a Victim

So what should you do if you ever become a victim of internet malfeasance? It happens to everyone eventually, even people like me who are experts at using the internet and practicing online safety. If you have read through this entire book you know that there are numerous ways you can protect yourself online, and you will also know that are numerous ways you can be victimized online as well. You will further recognize that some risks are fully beyond your control, such as when you buy something online and you trust the company to keep your credit card data safe.

Since many thousands of people are victimized online each day, it is important to know what to do should you ever become a victim. There are several steps and best practices to follow once you become a victim that will set you on the right path quickly and easily. If you act fast and **do not panic**, you can sometimes prevent any damage from being done whatsoever. To help demonstrate all of these points I am going to provide you with some examples, some of which have even happened to me.

Minimize the Damage

The very first thing you should do when you become a victim of an internet scam or fraud is *minimize the damage*. How you minimize the damage depends on how you became a victim in the first place. For instance, if you think your credit card details were stolen, the first thing you should do is call your credit card company and let them know. They can cancel your card immediately and prevent any fraudulent transactions from occurring. If you know for sure your credit card details were stolen, the very first thing you should do is again call the credit card company and have them disable your account and issue you a new card. By minimizing the damage in any online safety situation, you can sometimes prevent any serious consequences from occurring.

If your credit card details are compromised or stolen...

Call your credit card company immediately and let them know. They will take the appropriate action to secure your account.

If you have opened an email attachment that you now fear is dangerous...

Close the attachment immediately, and close any other programs that may have been affected by the attachment. Then delete the email and run a full virus scan using antivirus software.

If you think you have become a victim of a phishing email scam...

Report the email as spam and delete the email. Then change any passwords that may have been compromised from the phishing scam, and check to make sure none your account details have been changed, such as your recovery email address or phone number. You must also change your password for every other account that uses the same password that was compromised.

If your computer has started downloading a potentially malicious file that you do not want to download...

This can sometimes happen if you click on a suspicious link, and the link opens up a suspicious website and one or more files immediately begin downloading to your computer against your will. The first thing you should do is cancel all the current downloads, close your web browser, and then delete the downloaded files from your computer (they can usually be found in your Downloads folder). You should then consider running a full system scan with your antivirus software.

If you think one of your accounts have been hacked...

Change the password on the suspected account immediately and check to make sure no other account details have been altered. Some website accounts allow you to check your login history, so you can check that to see if anyone besides yourself has logged in to your account. You must also change your password for every other account that uses the same password that was compromised.

If you think your computer or device has been infected with a virus, spyware, adware, or malware...

Run a complete virus scan using antivirus software immediately. If the malware is making your computer unusable, you can boot the computer in safe mode or disconnect the internet connection to make it easier to use until you run the virus scan and clean out any malware.

If you have been defrauded through an online purchase you made at a website...

Contact the website first and make sure your concerns are correct. Ask them to please tell you what is going on with your order. If the company fails to respond in a reasonable amount of time or completely stonewalls you and acts suspicious, call your credit card company (or whichever financial company you used to make the purchase) and let them know what happened.

If you are a victim of ransomware...

Ransomware is a rare type of attack on individuals, but it does happen. If you are a victim of a ransomware attack you will not be able to access most or all of the files on your computer. When you try to open any file, you will see a message stating something like your system has been locked and in order to gain access to your files you will need to pay a ransom. The very first thing you should do in this situation is disconnect your computer from the internet, and then run a full virus scan to see if your antivirus software can clean it out. Unfortunately, antivirus software sometimes fails against ransomware, in which case your next option is to completely restore your computer to factory settings, which should delete everything on it including the ransomware. Hopefully you utilize a cloud backup service, in which case you can restore all of your deleted files from a *previous date in which your computer was not infected with the ransomware*.

If you have visited a website that is spamming your device making it hard to use...

For this type of instance I am talking about a website that spams your screen with popups, windows, messages indicating you have a virus, and other annoying content. When this happens, you should attempt to close down the website and your web browser, although this may be hard to do. If you cannot do this, force close your web browser by using the task manager on a Windows PC (control + alt + delete) or by force quitting on a Mac. Once you have successfully closed your browser, open it back up and clear your cookies and internet history. You also may want to run a full virus scan.

If one or more of your social media accounts was hacked...

Change your password for that social media account, and change any other passwords for accounts that use that particular password.

If you are being harassed or targeted for a scam by someone on social media...

Report and block the user on social media.

By taking the appropriate steps to minimize the damage in one of these situations you can possibly stop the attack before any real damage can occur. To demonstrate this, let's explore a couple of examples.

Example 1: Credit Card Details Stolen

This first example is an extremely common occurrence. In fact, it happened to me in 2018, and it was the second time I have had my credit card details stolen in ten years. At three in the morning, I received a surprise text message from my credit card company letting me know that a purchase I recently made was over my individual purchase limit I set as an alert. In the next few seconds, I received several more text messages notifying me of more high value purchases being made. At this point, it was obvious to me that something suspicious was going on, so the first thing I did was check to make sure I had my credit card in my possession, which I did. Next, I logged into my bank account online to look at my transaction history. Sure enough, just minutes ago several purchases were made within seconds of each other at various online stores for amounts ranging from $500 to $1500.

The next thing I did was call my credit card company using the number on the back of the card. I told them I wanted to report suspicious activity on my account, and they told me that their safeguards detected the unusual activity, and they stopped my credit card from being further used even before I called. They also told me that I would not be responsible for the fraudulent charges, and that they would be cancelling my current credit card and sending me a new one.

Let's review everything that happened here. First, it is important to recognize that I have suffered no financial damage because of this attack. My credit card company stopped further attacks from happening, and refunded me for all of the fraudulent charges. They knew the charges were fraudulent because the way the attack played out. My credit card was used halfway across the country and at online stores I never shop at, therefore it was easy for them to conclude that it was not me making the charges. Secondly, I did everything right by first checking to make sure the text messages were real by logging into my online account, and then calling the credit card company to let them know what was happening. In the end, the only damage I suffered was the inconvenience of having to make this phone call at three in the morning and having to wait a few days for a new credit card to arrive.

You may be wondering how my credit card details were stolen? I was wondering the same thing as well and unfortunately I was never able to discern how it happened. It is possible that I could have used my credit card on a fraudulent website, but that is highly unlikely as the card in question was only used at the same reputable websites and stores for many months. The more likely scenario is a company I used the card at was hacked, maybe even unknowingly, and the hacker was able to steal the credit card data of the company's customers including mine. Scenarios like this are somewhat common, and unfortunately it is unlikely that you will be able to determine how your credit card details were stolen in similar situations.

Example 2: Online Password Stolen

This next example is another common occurrence and has happened to me at least twice, with the most recent time being in 2017. Back in January of 2017, I received an email notifying me of a security breach at a news website I have an account at. The email stated that my account information, including email address and password, might have been compromised. The email urged me to change my password for my account, which I did on the news website that had the security breach. A couple of months later I received another email, this time from Google notifying me that suspicious activity was detected on my email account, and that they had taken action to prevent my account from being accessed. The email further stated that I needed to change my Google password immediately, which I then proceeded to do.

Before we go any further, let us examine what exactly happened here. This example starts off with me receiving an email from a news website I have an account with. The email states they had a security breach and that my account information is compromised and I should change my password. I followed their instructions and changed my password believing that was all that I needed to do to secure my account. A couple of months later, I find out someone tried to log in to my Google email address and that they had my password to do so, and I had to change that password as well. Could these two incidents be linked, or was it merely a coincidence?

It became obvious to me that these two incidents were explicitly linked, and that my own foolishness in not following the best practices of online safety led to my Google email address password being stolen. But how? How could a security breach for my online account for a news website lead to my Google email address being hacked? The answer is simple, and it revolves around online password security that is covered in the next chapter: the hacker used my account information for the news website and attempted to use that same information for other websites.

Here is a breakdown of how the hacker was able to access my Google email account. When I created an account for the news website, I used my Gmail email address as the account username. Then, when I created a password for this account, I used the same password that I use for nearly all of my online accounts, including my email address.

Then, when the hacker stole my information from the news website, they now could see my account username (which was my email address) and my account password (which was the same password I use for all of my accounts). The hacker then tried to log in to my Google email address using the password he hacked from the news website. He was right in assuming that I used the same password for nearly all of my accounts, so technically he had my password for just about everything.

Fortunately, Google prevented the hacker from logging in to my account. They were able to do this because the hacker tried to log in at a location I have never been at before. If the hacker was able to log in, he then would have had access to all of my emails, which he can further use to cause me harm. He could have used my emails to see where I have other online accounts, such as banks and social media. He then could have logged into any of those accounts using my email address, even if I did have a separate password for those accounts, because he could have simply reset my password and a had a new password sent to my email address which he now has access to.

The moral of the story leads to this best practice:

> **Best Practice:** If one of your online accounts or passwords is stolen or compromised, change the password for that account and any other account that uses that password.

If I would have changed my password for all of my accounts that use the password that was stolen, this situation could have easily been prevented.

Fortify your Defenses

If you become a victim of an online fraud, attack, or scam, after minimizing the damage and resolving the issue the next step you should take is to fortify your defenses so you are better protected from that type of attack in the future. So if you were a victim of a phishing email or a virus, you should consider getting antivirus software installed on your computer to prevent the same type of attack. If your online password was stolen, you should start practicing the online password best practices to protect yourself in the future. Lastly, if you are being personally targeted or harassed on social media, you should consider making your account private or blocking people who are bothering you.

Chapter 11 – Tips & Tricks

Congratulations! You have made it through the majority of this book, and you now have the tools and knowledge necessary to use the internet safely on all of your device. The internet is so vast and untamed that is impossible to cover all of the risks you can face online, but we have covered many of the most common aspects that you may encounter. Moreover, most of the best practices of this book have universal and far-reaching benefits, meaning that when they are followed they can protect you from most of the threats you can face online in any situation. In this last chapter, we are going to cover some meaningful tips and tricks that will help aide you in your quest to use the internet safely.

Online Password Safety

This section is the most important of this chapter, and covers the many aspects of creating and using online passwords safely and securely. Your online passwords are the lock and key to all of your digital information, and protecting your sensitive information online is a very important element of online safety. The best practices outlined in this section will provide you with some of the best security measures you can take, while also considering feasibility so that you are not labored with onerous password measures.

Best Practice: First, create a unique universal password that you will easily remember. This will be your standard password.

This is the first step in creating a password system for yourself that you will eventually build off of. This unique password should be something you can easily remember, and should contain the following:

- At least 8 characters long
- Contains a mix of numbers and letters, not conveniently placed at the beginning or end

What you want to do here is create your standard password that you can always fall back on. You will not be using this password on every account, however you will utilize this password in certain ways for most of your accounts. As an example, let's say I want my standard password to reflect my love of baseball and my favorite number, which is 42. So I may think to create a standard password of "baseball42". This is a good start, however this is not an ideal choice since a password like this can be easily guessed. A better choice would be to place the 42 in the middle of the word, so "base42ball". This is a much better choice than the first, however it is still not ideal. An ideal password would not have full common words inside it, so one technique you can follow is to replace some of the letters of the words with comparable numbers. For this case, let's replace the A's in the password with the number "4", which is sometimes used to represent the letter A. So now we have, "b4se42b4ll". This is a strong standard password that meets all of the criteria specified. Remember, we just want to create a standard password that we can build upon later, and for this example, "b4se42b4ll" fits the bill. (Other numbers that can reflect letters are 1 = I or L, 3 = E, 4 = A, 5 = S, 6 = G, 7 = T, 8 = B, and 0 = O.)

Once you have created a standard password, write it down somewhere safe and try to memorize it. This will be the password that you rely on to create all of your other passwords. Obviously, do not use the exact password in this example since many people will have read this book.

Best Practice: Create a document where you will record and keep all of your passwords.

You can do this either on paper or in an Excel or Word document on your computer. I suggest using an Excel document, as you can print it and password protect the document itself so others cannot view it. If you want to use a paper document, Infinity Guides has some excellent password ledgers for sale on www.infinityguides.com. In this document you are going to have four columns: account, username, password, and notes. In the account column will be the website or service for your account, such as Yahoo, Google, Chase Bank, or some other company. You can also enter the web address in this column if you prefer. In the username column, you should enter the exact username you use to login to your account. In the password column, you are going to list your password, however we are going to do it a little differently.

Inside the password column is where you will be recording all of the passwords for all of your different accounts. A document like this is necessary since different accounts require different password specifications. Some websites may require that your password contain both upper and lowercase letters, along with numbers and symbols. These passwords will differ from your standard password, and you will need to note these differences in the password column. I personally do not like to ever write my standard password on an electronic or paper document; instead, I write "standard" in the password column whenever I use my standard password for an account. For accounts where I am required to add a symbol, I simply add the symbol to the beginning, middle, or end of my standard password and I always use the same symbol. So I could make my altered standard password, "#b4se42b4ll", "b4se42#b4ll", or "b4se42b4ll#". Then, on my passwords document, I write "#standard, stand#ard, or standard#", which indicates where I placed the hashtag on my standard password. The same principle applies for passwords that require capital and lower case letters:

- standarD – indicates my standard password with last letter capitalized (b4se42b4lL)
- Standard – indicates my standard password with the first letter capitalized (B4se42b4ll)
- Standard# - indicates my standard password with the first letter capitalized and the # symbol added to the end (B4se42b4ll#)

The whole point of writing standard is because only I know my standard password, and I never want a documented record of that password available to anyone. I also know that I personally will never forget my standard password, therefore I am completely comfortable writing standard instead of the password itself.

For accounts where you do not use your standard password or any variation of it, you should just write the exact password you are using. Lastly, if you create a Word or Excel document to store your passwords, you should password protect that document using your standard password. To do this, when you go to save the file, go to <u>Tools</u> and then <u>General Options</u>, and then enter your standard password for the read and modify options (<u>Figure 11.1</u>).

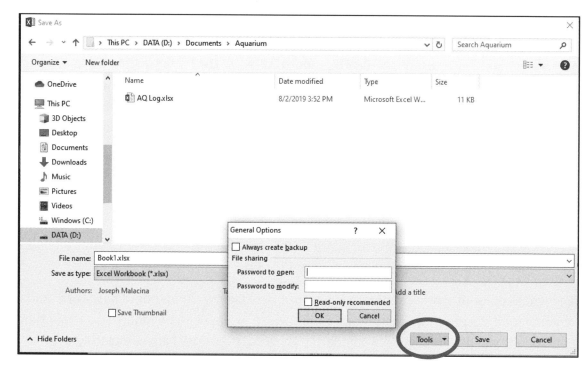

Figure 11.1– Password Protecting a Word or Excel Document

Best Practice: If you have more than 3 online accounts, then you should not use the same password for all of these accounts.

This best practice is both about convenience and security. Ideally, you would want to have a unique password for every single one of your online accounts. For most people however, this is too cumbersome and unreasonable, and so they will try to use the same password for each account. In my opinion, using the same password for each account is only acceptable if you have three online accounts or less. This way, if your password for any of your accounts is ever stolen, you would need to change your password for all of your accounts, and since you have less than four, it would not take you too long to do so. If you do in fact use the same password for all of your accounts, please keep in mind that if your password is ever stolen then that thief could potentially have access to all of your accounts.

If you do have more than three online accounts, then you should employ some variation to your standard password for each account. There are several different ways you can do this, and I like to recommend ways that are simple and easy to remember. One such way is to add a letter to your standard password that corresponds with the website the account is associated with. For instance, if you have a Yahoo account, you can add the letter Y to your password in a convenient location. Or, if you have a Google account, you can add the letter G to a convenient location in your standard password. Better yet, you could use the first two letters of Google, "GO", and add that to your password instead of just one letter. I do not recommend adding the entire name of the website to your password. You should of course note any variation of your standard password in your passwords document:

- standardy – indicates my standard password with the letter **y** added to the end, perhaps for my Yahoo account (b4se42b4lly)
- Ystandard# - indicates my standard password with a **capital y** added to the beginning, and the **# symbol** added to the end, perhaps for my Yahoo account (Yb4se42b4ll#)
- Standard#G - indicates my standard password with the **first letter capitalized**, the **# symbol** added to the end, and the **capital G** added to the very end, perhaps for my Google account (B4se42b4ll#G)

Best Practice: Make use of password remembrance tools on devices and browsers.

Most web browsers come with tools that will remember and autofill your passwords for you. Some mobile devices have this feature as well. The way this works is your browser or device will take note the first time you login to a website and it will save your password for you in an encrypted database. Then, the next time you visit the website and you need to login, your browser will fill in your username and password for you.

This is different from another web browser tool, known as the password generator. This tool generates a unique password for you whenever you attempt to create an account on a website. This password is usually a random collection of numbers, letters, and symbols that would be extremely difficult to hack. Your browser will remember this password and fill it in for you whenever you visit the website. The only issue with this tool is that it will only work when you are using that particular web browser. If you switch to another device and use a different web browser, you will not be able to easily access that generated password. Furthermore, if you ever forget your password for the account you use on your web browser, you may have a very hard time accessing these generated passwords.

Best Practice: Never use easily guessable passwords or passwords that can be easily identified to you.

This should be common sense, however research has shown that even today, the most popular password people use is the word "password". Moreover, many people use the PIN number "1234" or "1111". This is completely unacceptable for a password or PIN and you should never, under any circumstances, use the word "password" as your actual password. The first word hackers are going to try when attempting to hack any account may very well be the word "password" and its many variations. You also should not use your name, address, or birthdate in your password as these can be easily guessed as well.

When creating a PIN for access to your mobile device (lock screen security), I would recommend you go with a 6-digit PIN rather than 4-digits. 4-digit PINs are more common, however they provide little security for brute force attacks. A brute force attack is an attempt to crack your PIN by entering every possible combination via software or a tool. So for a 4 digit PIN with no additional security protocols, a brute force attack can try all 10,000 combinations in about 500 minutes (assuming it could enter one PIN every 3 seconds). A 6-digit PIN has 1,000,000 possible combinations, and thus would take 50,000 minutes to attempt every possible combination. Fortunately, most devices have additional security protocols that prevent most brute force type attacks from being successful. For one, a brute force attack on your mobile device can generally only be attempted if the attacker has physical possession of your device. Secondly, many devices allow only a set number of attempts before the device will completely shut itself down to prevent further attempts. Regardless, if you value your privacy and data on your device, than you should use a 6-digit PIN or full password as your lock screen security.

Brute force attacks are rare on personal accounts, but they do sometimes happen. You are more likely to be targeted by a brute force attack if you are a high value target, such as a politician, corporate executive, or wealthy individual. If you consider yourself a high value target, then you should take the most care when creating all of your passwords and PINs. At a minimum, all of your passwords should be at least 8 characters long, should contain multiple symbols and numbers, and should utilize both upper and lowercase letters.

Best Practice: Never share your online passwords with anyone through any medium.

You should never, under any circumstances, tell your password to someone over the phone who you do not trust. You should never, under any circumstances, write your password in an email and send it. If anyone asks for your account password through email or over the phone, you absolutely should not give it to them and immediately consider them suspicious. The only time you would provide information like this over the phone is if you have an additional PIN or account password set up with the account. For instance, some companies allow you to create an additional verbal password in order to verify your identity or confirm changes. These passwords are different than your normal login password and are okay to share if you called and intended to do so. On the other hand, passwords of any sort should never be sent over email.

Best Practice: Create a secondary password that you will use on websites you do not particularly trust.

You should create and have a secondary password that is easy for you to remember and is completely separate and unrelated to your standard password. You will only be using this password on websites you do not consider trustworthy or have a history of security breaches. That way, if your notions about the untrustworthy website are true, then only your secondary password was stolen and your main standard password and all its variations remain completely safe. You should not use this secondary password on any important websites such as your bank, primary social media accounts, or your email accounts.

Craigslist Safety

This section of this chapter has been added by popular demand, and deals with using the Craigslist.org website, or any similar classifieds website. Craigslist is the classifieds website of the internet, and is comparable to the classifieds page of a newspaper. People use Craigslist to buy and sell local items, look for work, hire contractors, rent apartments, and discuss random topics online. The website is very popular in the United States and Canada, and the site itself is a reflection of the libertarian attitude of the internet. With that being said, Craigslist attracts many scammers and frauds, and acute caution should be exercised by anyone using the website.

If you plan on using the Craigslist.org website, you should be well versed in the many aspects of online safety covered in this book. Craigslist is a great website for selling old items or finding good deals, but it is also a hotbed for fraud, scams, and crime. I will cover some specific practices you can utilize to protect yourself when using Craigslist (or any similar classifieds website), however I recommend that you be highly attuned to the best practices covered throughout this book, as you will no doubt come across numerous scams on the Craigslist website.

Communicating on Craigslist

With Craigslist, you normally communicate with a poster through email. For instance, a user may make a post about a cell phone for sale. If you wanted to contact the person to express your interest in the phone, you would click on the email button and you would then be able to email that person. *When emailing someone on Craigslist, use your secondary (online identity email) and be sure to use the anonymous email relay function on Craigslist.* This is important to do because there are many scammers on Craigslist who are just trying to collect email addresses that they can package together into a spam list. When you use the anonymous email function on craigslist, your email address will be hidden from view. This however, will not hide the name you have linked to your email address; which is why you should use your secondary or online identity email instead of your primary email address.

Typically, after some email communication between you and another Craigslist user takes place, one of you might suggest texting for future conversations. This usually makes communication easier especially if you are planning on meeting to exchange money for goods. *If you decide to communicate with a Craigslist user over text message, I recommend that you use a third-party texting app instead of your actual phone number.* Examples of third-party texting apps include Whatsapp, GroupMe, Textfree, and WeChat. This is simply a safety precaution that you should take when dealing with strangers on Craigslist.

Be Prepared for Anything

As stated earlier, many people use Craigslist to buy and sell used goods or to exchange services. I have personally used Craigslist to sell old cell phones, hire temporary workers, and buy sports tickets, and the examples I will provide will show you exactly what you can expect to deal with when using Craigslist. In my own personal experience, about 70% of the interactions I have had on Craigslist where genuine, and 30% were fraudulent or sketchy at best. Twice, I have used Craigslist to hire temporary workers to move some boxes. The first time I hired workers, the people were great. The second time I hit bad luck, and the workers were very lazy and constantly asking for more money.

In another instance, I used Craigslist to sell my old cell phone. As is typical on Craigslist, the first offers I received were well below what I was asking. When I finally found someone willing to pay my price, things did not go as planned. We decided to meet at public place where the buyer would pay in cash and I would sell them the phone. When we met, the buyer only had half the cash that we agreed to, and told me that was all he had and I should just take it and do the deal. When I refused to do the deal, the buyer started yelling and making a scene, at which point I just walked away, only losing about half an hour of my time. Later on I found another buyer who agreed to my price and we had a pleasant transaction. This experience of selling my cell phone is a good example of how your dealings can go with strangers you meet on the website.

Another example of a Craigslist interaction worth discussing is one that happened to a good friend of mine. She was trying to sell her cell phone on Craigslist, and found a buyer who would pay her price. They agreed to meet at a coffee shop in town, and everything was set to go. When the time came to meet, she went to the coffee shop alone and sat at a table. She provided the buyer with a description of her appearance so he could identify her when he arrived. When the buyer did in fact arrive, he did not come alone. Instead, he showed up with two other men and walked right up to her, grabbed the cell phone from her hands and ran out of the coffee shop.

Another Craigslist example that went astray is one that happened to another friend of mine, who was using the site to purchase concert tickets. He found a buyer who was willing to sell two of his tickets for a reasonable price. My friend met the buyer at a public place, paid cash for the tickets, and took the tickets home with him. A couple of days later, my friend went to the concert, and when he attempted to use the tickets to enter the venue, he was denied entry. The venue stated that the concert tickets were cancelled by the owner, and that his tickets were invalid. There was nothing he could do, and he was out the money for the tickets and could not attend the sold-out show. It was hard to see this coming, as the tickets he bought from the Craigslist stranger were in fact real tickets in shape and size, however the seller pulled a scam on my friend by cancelling the tickets and requesting new ones, thus making those tickets worthless. My friend had no recourse, as Craigslist is anonymous and he did not know the identity of the seller.

The last example I am going to share is one that happened to a colleague of mine. He was using Craigslist to buy tickets to a sporting event. He found a seller who was selling two tickets for a reasonable price and agreed to purchase them. They communicated first through email, and then through text message. The seller stated that the tickets were digital, and that he would send the tickets to my colleague via email the moment he received payment. He wanted payment through a payment app such as Venmo, Zelle, or Cash app. When my acquaintance paid the seller, he never heard from him again, and there was no way he could get his money back.

All of these examples demonstrate the wide array of risks and rewards you can encounter when using Craigslist. They will also help us derive some best practices you can follow to protect yourself from potential scammers.

Best Practice: If you are going to meet a stranger from Craigslist for a transaction, meet in a safe, public place with security cameras.

You should never meet someone on Craigslist in your home or theirs. You also do not want to meet on a street corner or in a secluded place. Instead, pick a place that is highly public, has security cameras, and is unlikely for a crime to occur. The best place I have ever used to meet a Craigslist stranger is a police station that allowed people to meet there for such transactions. I have also used grocery stores, banks, and museums as meeting spots. I have found that scammers will generally refuse to meet in such secure places or will just not show up.

Best Practice: If buying or selling something from a Craigslist stranger, agree on a price before you meet

This is great practice to follow to make sure your eventual meeting goes smoothly. If you are a buyer, make sure the price you agreed to pay is set in stone before you meet the seller. Let them know that you will only bring the amount agreed upon. If you are the seller, let the buyer know that the price is final and you will not accept less when you meet. The only time you might accept less is if the buyer finds that the item you are selling is damaged or not as advertised when you meet.

Best Practice: Never pay for an item until you meet in person, and only pay in cash or through a payment app

Cash or payment through an app should be the only acceptable payment methods when transacting through Craigslist. Keep in mind that any payment you make or receive through an app, such as Venmo, Zelle, Cash app, or Chase Quickpay is final and cannot be cancelled or recovered. It is essentially the same as handing someone cash and you should treat it as such. Hence, why it is so important that you **never** pay for an item until the item is in your possession. If you are the seller of an item and the buyer is paying in cash, you might want to invest in a counterfeit-checking marker to make sure the cash they are paying you with is legitimate, especially if it is a large amount of cash.

Best Practice: When buying an item, always inspect an item thoroughly before finalizing the transaction

It is not unheard of on Craigslist for sellers to be selling fake, fraudulent, or counterfeit merchandise to unsuspecting buyers, and you should always use due diligence when purchasing an item. I recommend you view each item for sale on Craigslist with a great deal of skepticism, especially if the item is an antique or valuable artifact. You should also use extreme caution when purchasing tickets to venues, as it can be impossible to verify that the tickets are legitimate.

Best Practice: Always put your safety first when communicating or meeting with someone on Craigslist

This is the most important best practice as it has to do with your personal safety. If you are uncomfortable with the thought of meeting a stranger from Craigslist, then do not do it. The fact is you never know who is on the other side of that email or text message, and you should prioritize your safety over the great deal you might be getting. If you do plan on meeting someone from Craigslist, there are additional steps you can take to try and protect yourself:

- If possible, try to verify each other's identity through Facebook before meeting.
- Try to investigate the person you are about to meet through their social media accounts and a web search.
- Bring a friend along to the meeting, but do not meet the person with your friend next to you, as this might make the other person very uncomfortable.
- If the person you are meeting insists on bringing a friend, you should bring one as well.

When I converse with someone on Craigslist, I always make my safety intentions very clear from the outset. I specify that I will only meet in a public place, and that the buyer or seller must add me as a friend on Facebook first so I can check them out and decide for myself if they are safe. Facebook is the best social media platform to use for this purpose as it is very difficult for someone to create a fake profile on it (see Chapter 5 for how to identify a fake profile on Facebook). Only after I have checked them out thoroughly and decided they are a safe person will I agree to meet with them for a transaction.

Online Jargon

The internet has its own culture, sense of community, and customs that may seem foreign to someone who is not familiar with them. In this section I will attempt to familiarize you with some of these aspects to help you better understand and use the internet.

Grammar Rules

The digital world has varying degrees of rules when it comes to using proper grammar. In some spaces, using correct grammar and punctuation are expected, and in others it is completely nonexistent. In general, I have found the following to be true:

- All digital communication in a professional manner should use correct grammar and punctuation.
- Email messages should use correct grammar.
- Text messages, in general, do not require proper grammar.
- Social media posts, in general, do not require proper grammar. Some platforms encourage better grammar than others. Facebook typically has proper grammar whereas Twitter has little proper grammar.
- Comments on websites and social media rarely have proper grammar, as space is limited and you need to get your point across with as little space as possible
- Online forums can go either way in terms of grammar. It completely depends on the type of forum.

Memes

An internet meme is hard to define with a sentence or two. The best way to describe a meme would be to call it a piece of content that is meant provide a message or humor that is subsequently shared by others. Usually, a meme will take the form of an image or video snippet (called a GIF) with a piece of text attached to it. Memes are immensely popular, and can often be found on social media platforms and online forums. Here is an example of what a meme typically looks like (Figure 11.2).

<u>Figure 11.2</u>– **Example of a Meme (image with text)**

Some General Internet Terms

<u>Troll</u> – A troll is a person online who instigates disagreement just for fun. They often try to anger people by poking fun at them.

<u>Bump</u> – Bump is a termed used on online forums to try and "bump" the topic higher on the forum's list. When you see a post with just the word bump, the person is trying to push the post higher on the forum so it will get more attention and engagement.

<u>Noob</u> – Noob is the short form of the word newbie, and is often used on social media and online gaming.

Acronyms

The internet makes use of a plethora of acronyms, especially on social media, texting, and messaging apps. For a list of common acronyms used on the internet, see Appendix I in the back of this book.

Off The Grid

This special section is for those who want to take their online privacy to the absolute extreme, and want to make sure none of their data is collected in any way, shape, or form. For the average person, this section will have little use to you, and if you have no interest in staying off the grid then you can completely skip this section. For the preppers, government conspiracy theorists, and privacy knights, this section will be pure gold, as I will show you to stay completely off the grid when using the internet. Following these recommendations will give you the most privacy and anonymity possible by my standards, although nothing is 100% foolproof and if you truly want to be off the grid then you might not want to use the internet at all. Anyways, let's begin.

Use a Virtual Private Network (VPN)

If you want to be off the grid, the very first thing you should utilize is a VPN on all of your devices, including your computers, smartphones, and tablets. A VPN is a virtual private network that routes all of your internet traffic through another server. In other words, it is a computer in a completely separate location that links to your device and routes all of the information that you send and receive through its server, and then out into the internet. What this does is mask the identity of your device and replaces it with the identity of the VPN. So if you are browsing a website on your phone without a VPN, the website and your internet provider can see the unique address of your device and see which website it is currently connected to. Anything you do on that website can be tracked back to the unique address of your device, and therefore back to you. When using a VPN, the website and your internet provider normally cannot see your device's unique address. Instead, they see the unique address of the VPN, which may be in a completely different location and being used by several people at once. Therefore, they cannot link the activity of the VPN to your device specifically, thus making your activity essentially anonymous.

VPNs come in many different shapes and sizes, and all are not perfect. All VPNs will slow your internet speed as you will be routing your traffic through another server, and some VPNs will slow your speed more than others. The best VPNs are ones you typically have to pay for, and my personal recommendation is NordVPN, which is extremely easy to use. You should make sure you have the VPN enabled for all of your devices and that it is always enabled.

Always Use Private Browsing

If you want you to stay off the grid, you must make sure you are always using private browsing on your web browser. Your VPN should be sufficient enough to cover this, but the additional security of using private browsing in your web browser will make your data even more private. The less data websites can collect from you the better, and with both a VPN and private browsing enabled, the websites you visit will have absolutely no clue who you are. You will notice this when you start seeing advertisements that you positively have no interest in. My personal recommendation for a web browser to best keep you off the grid is the Brave browser with private browsing always enabled.

Never agree to cookies, never allow apps or devices to collect data, and disable location tracking

These three recommendations are essential if you are going to stay completely off the grid. When you are using private browsing, you are already blocking most cookies from being collected from you. Cookies are snippets of web data that remember your browsing activity to provide you with a better browsing experience. On occasion, you will come across websites that ask you to accept their policy of collecting cookies. You should reject this request as it could be an end-around into collecting data from you, especially if you do not have a VPN or private browsing enabled.

In addition, many apps and devices also try to collect data from you in order to "fix bugs and provide better updates". Most people allow their apps and devices to collect this data without thinking, but you want to stay off the grid, therefore you should never allow an app to collect data from you. With some apps, it may not be possible to prevent it from collecting data, and that is okay as long as you follow all of the other recommendations in this section. Most devices try and collect diagnostic data from you as well, and they will ask you if you want to allow this during the initial setup of the device. Deny their request and use your device with the peace of mind that they cannot see a speck of your activity.

Lastly, and this is the most important of these three recommendations, you need to be sure that location tracking is disabled on your device. Even when you are using a VPN, many devices do not rely on your internet connection to check your location. Instead, they use the GPS location of your device, which is separate from your internet connection. Your VPN does not mask this GPS marker and you can only block it by disabling it through your device's settings. You want to make sure that location tracking is disabled for your device as a whole, and that each app you have installed on your device is not allowed to access your location. The Apple iPhone is a particularly great device for managing your location tracking settings. (See Chapter 6 on how to disable location tracking on an Apple or Android device.)

Use third-party apps with encryption for all of your direct communication

If you want to stay off the grid, you cannot use your smartphone's native cell service to make phone calls or send text messages. Simply put, if you use your cellular provider's native systems to make a call or send a text, they will have a record of that call or text, and could actually have your text messages' content. Fortunately, there are a host of third party apps that allow you to send messages and make calls with complete privacy. These apps encrypt your messages and calls end-to-end, which make them impossible to intercept and to be monitored by others. The Apple iPhone does this with its iMessage feature, which is text messages you send and receive to and from other Apple device users. Some third-party apps I recommend that also encrypt their messages and calls are: Facebook Messenger (using secret messages) and WhatsApp.

You should also be sure the email provider you are using encrypts your email messages end-to-end. Most email providers do not do this, and instead use basic encryption such as SSL/TLS. With only SSL/TLS encryption, your provider has the encryption keys so they can technically decrypt your emails. With end-to-end encryption, only the sender and receiver can read the email messages, and it is an extremely secure way to keep your emails completely off the grid. Email providers that offer end-to-end encryption generally charge a monthly fee for use, and my recommendation is ProtonMail.

Do not use the cloud for backup purposes, and do not use any facial scanning or fingerprint scanning lock screen technology on your devices

It is completely okay if your devices have the capability for facial or fingerprint scanning, however you should not be using these as a security measure to lock your device if you want to stay off the grid. Locking your device means setting up a passcode or security measure that must be addressed in order for someone to use the device. In most cases, people use a PIN and biometric scanning technology to lock their device. To unlock it, they simply need to look at their device, place their fingerprint on it, or enter their PIN. The off the grid person will only set a PIN or password, and they will make sure that PIN is at least six digits long. If you were to use facial or fingerprint scanning as your lock screen security, then anyone can access your device by placing your finger on it or placing it in front of your face, and that is not good policy. So make sure you utilize a PIN or password only, and make sure your password is a good one.

Furthermore, you must make sure you are not using the cloud to backup any of your devices if you truly want to stay off the grid. As you know from reading this book, some devices (such as the Apple iPhone and iPad) cannot be accessed by anyone except the owner with the lock screen passcode. Not even government agencies can get into these devices if they do not know the passcode (to the best of my knowledge). These agencies can however, with relative ease via subpoena, access your cloud backup if you utilize one. That means they can access your email, apps, photos, contacts, videos, call logs, and maybe even your text messages if they are backed up in the cloud. If you do not use the cloud as a backup, then your data is truly protected from any unauthorized intrusion.

Do not use voice-enabled smart assistants or voice recognition on your devices...

I am talking of course about the digital assistants many devices have that you can speak to, and they follow your command. Many of these devices claim that their artificial voice helpers are completely safe and secure, but in my opinion the jury is still out on this technology. These voice assistants are connected to the internet, and use what you say to deliver you information. There is no way to tell if your device may be listening to you when you are not using the assistant, and if you truly want to be off the grid this is a risk you cannot take. Therefore, you should disable the voice assistant through your device's settings so you can be sure your device is never listening in on your private conversations.

Learn about cryptocurrency

Cryptocurrency is a digital currency designed for the digital world. Its purpose is to take government out of the money supply, and it is designed with privacy in mind. Cryptocurrency is a risky business, so I will not provide advice on whether you should invest in it or not. However, for those who truly want to stay off the grid, cryptocurrency can be very appealing as a means of currency. Many online stores accept cryptocurrency as a form of payment, and it is relatively easy to trade popular cryptocurrencies, such as Bitcoin, for American Dollars or Euros.

By following the recommendations in this section, you will have successfully made yourself off the grid on the internet in many ways. Enjoy being invisible and anonymous on the internet, and keep in mind that nothing is 100% guaranteed in terms of online privacy.

Chapter 12 – Conclusion & More Resources

Thank you for reading *Online Safety: The Complete Guide to Being Safe Online*. It is my hope that you are now fully prepared and educated on the many aspects of online safety, and that you now feel confident about using the internet on all of your devices. In fact, I am personally confident that if you took the time to read this entire book, then you will have no problem using the internet safely and wisely. Continue to use this book as a reference when you need it. The Table of Contents can quickly lead you to your answer for pressing issues.

I welcome your thoughts and feedback on this book. Please come visit my social media pages online and send me a message if you so desire. I am often found online answering questions and chatting with readers of my books to help them with their technology needs. As a last piece of advice, please remember to utilize the best practices of this book. These practices alone will provide you with a strong foundation for using the internet safely. Furthermore, please never forget the #1 Rule of Social Media, as it will be your guiding principle when using social media.

Enjoy using the internet on all of your devices, and stay safe.

More Resources

This book has covered many of the aspects of online safety for your devices, including computers, smartphones, and tablets. Online safety is constantly evolving, and new types of risks and threats are constituted each and every year. To stay up to date on the latest news, threats, and safety reports, subscribe to my personal newsletter at www.joemalacina.com. I write an email article to my 50,000+ subscribers about twice a month about technology, social media, and the internet in general.

You can also follow me on social media for news, advice, and to get in touch me. I can be reached on most social media platforms:

- **Facebook:** Visit www.facebook.com/joemalacina1 or search for Joe Malacina
- **Twitter:** Follow @JoeMalacina or visit www.twitter.com/joemalacina
- **Instagram:** Follow me @JoeMal26 or visit www.instagram.com/joemal26

There is a lot more you can learn about technology, online safety, and social media in general. If you consider yourself a beginner in any of these topics, I recommend you check out **Infinity Guides**, which is an online resource for beginners where you can find educational online courses, books, manuals, and DVDs. They have content covering social media, smartphones, tablets, and computers in general.

www.infinityguides.com Content:

- *Facebook for Beginners*
- *Twitter for Beginners*
- *Instagram for Beginners*
- *Snapchat for Beginners*
- *Smartphones & Tablets for Beginners*
- *Mac Computer for Beginners*
- *iTunes for Beginners*
- *Apple Music for Beginners*
- *Complete Guide to Cleaning up your Computer*

Appendix A – Common Online Acronyms

- AF – As f-word
- AFK – Away from keyboard
- ASL – What is your age, sex, and location?
- ATM – At the moment
- Bae – Boyfriend or girlfriend (not an acronym)
- BBL – Be back later
- BF – Boyfriend
- BFF – Best friend forever
- BRB – Be right back
- BTW – By the way
- DD – Dear daughter (referring to your own daughter)
- DH – Dear husband
- DIY – Do it yourself
- DM – Direct message
- DS – Dear son (referring to your own son)
- DW – Dear wife
- FB - Facebook
- FML – F-word my life
- FTFY – Fixed that for you
- FWB – Friends with benefits
- FYI – For your information
- GF – Girlfriend
- GOAT – Greatest of all time
- GTFO – Get the freak out
- HMU – Hit me up
- HRU – How are you?
- IDC – I don't care
- IDK – I don't know
- IIRC – If I remember correctly
- IKR - I know, right?
- IMHO – In my honest/humble opinion
- IMO – In my opinion
- IRL – In real life
- JK – Just kidding
- LMFAO – Laughing my freaking a** off
- LMK – Let me know
- LOL – Laughing out loud
- MRW – My reaction when
- NBD – No big deal
- NMU – Not much, you?
- NP – No Problem
- NSFW – Not safe for work
- NVM – Never mind
- OMG – Oh my God
- OMW – On my way
- OP – Original poster
- PAH – Parents a home
- PAP – Post a photo
- PAW – Parents are watching
- POV – Point of view
- RN – Right now
- ROFL – Rolling on floor laughing
- RT – Retweet
- SMH – Shaking my head
- STFU – Shut the f-word up
- TBH – To be honest
- TFW – That feeling when…
- TIL – Today I learned
- TL;DR – Too long, didn't read
- TMI – Too much information

- TTYL – Talk to you later
- TY – Thank you
- WFH – Working from home
- WTF – What the f-word
- WTH – What the Hell?
- YOLO – You only live once
- YW – You're welcome

Appendix B – List of Best Practices

WEB BROWSING

- When deciding on a web browser, use one of the major and trusted browsers listed in Chapter 2. These browsers are reliable, secure, and are compatible with nearly every website. Furthermore, whichever web browser you choose, use that same browser across all of your devices if you can.
- Most of the time, you will be just fine browsing the internet normally without private browsing. In fact, browsing the internet in private mode can make using some websites difficult. However, you should use private browsing whenever you do not want your activity and history to be collected and shared.
- Whenever you are in doubt about an advertisement, visualize whatever the advertisement is telling in you in a real life situation, such as a random person on the street coming up to you and saying the exact thing to you that the advertisement is stating. This will help you put the ad in perspective and allow you to make a better choice on whether to indulge the ad.
- Only use an ad blocker extension if you find yourself overwhelmed with advertisements that interfere with your ability to browse the web. This best practice does not apply if you use the Brave browser, which blocks all ads by default.
- If you ever suspect that a recommendation is **only** being made to you online for financial gain, and not for genuine purposes, hover your mouse over the link to see the URL, and look to see if it contains several unordered numbers and letters. If it does, your suspicions may be right and you should consider doing additional research. Remember, even if the link is a paid referral, it does not necessarily mean the content is disingenuous.
- If you suspect an article may be clickbait, it probably is. Don't waste your time clicking on something that triggered a significant emotional response for the sake of getting your reaction. Ignore the headline and move on. Most clickbait articles have a misleading headline anyways.
- Always use caution whenever you are asked to divulge personal information on the internet. The less information you give out, the better. If you ever find yourself in doubt as to whether you should provide information to a website, ask a trusted friend or better yet ask me: you can always write to me on Facebook

(@JoeMalacina1 / www.facebook.com/joemalacina1) or Twitter (@JoeMalacina / www.twitter.com/joemalacina) and I will give you my best advice.

ONLINE SHOPPING

- When shopping online, always do a quick check in your web browser to see if the website has an SSL certificate **while you are on the payment details page**. If the website does not have an SSL certificate (known as not secure), do not enter any payment details unless you are paying using a third-party payer such as PayPal, that will have SSL security.
- When purchasing goods or services online, ALWAYS use a credit card or third-party payer to complete payment. NEVER use a debit card, electronic check, or ACH bank transfer.
- Use a third-party payer, such as PayPal, when purchasing something from a website that you do not particularly trust.
- Create a folder in your email account and name it "Receipts". Move all receipts you receive through email into this folder and keep them for at least six months.

EMAIL

- Always check links in suspicious or urgent emails that are urging you to disclose sensitive information such as your password. Be sure the links are directing you to the correct website with the correct domain.
- Always examine a link or URL in a suspicious email. Make sure the URL of the link is directing you to the proper domain, and beware of URLs that are designed to fool you.
- Do not open attachments from any email you consider suspicious. If in doubt, only open attachments from senders you are *expecting* to receive an attachment from.
- Never, under any circumstances, open an attachment that has a file extension of .exe, .iso, or .bat.
- If you do open an attachment that is suspicious, examine any links inside the attachment for domain accuracy. Be wary of any attachment files that direct you to click on a link.
- If you receive an email that is too good to be true, it probably is. Always treat a suspicious email as if a stranger on the street came up to you and said the exact content of the email to your face. That will help you put it in perspective.

- When you come across an email that is directing you to change your password or login to your account, examine the links in the email for the proper domain.
- Consider any email that directs you to reset your password or login to your account as suspicious **if** you were not expecting to receive that email.
- If you receive a *suspicious* email that directs you to reset your password or login to your account, go to the supposed website manually instead of clicking on any links within the email.
- Never open an attachment in an email message from an unknown sender, and if you do open it, then do not click on any links inside the attachment. Never, under any circumstances, open an attachment that has the file extension types .exe, .iso, and .bat.
- If you come across a suspicious email, never use the from email name and email address as way to authenticate the email's legitimacy.
- Follow the recommended naming conventions for your personal email address, and use a second email address for your online identity.
- Do not use your Internet Service Provider for your email address

SOCIAL MEDIA

- Always remember the #1 Rule of Social Media: There is no such thing as privacy when using social media, and anything you share on social media will <u>forever</u> will be public.
- Before making any type of post to social media, always keep in mind that whatever you post can never truly be deleted.
- A private social media account is still susceptible to having its information become public. Therefore, you should treat all of your social media profiles as if everyone in the public can see its information.
- If you want to make sure your private messages exchanged through social media are kept safe and secure, make sure the people you are conversing with are well-versed on online safety. If they are not, buy them this book.
- **Facebook:** Never share any of your passwords through Facebook Messenger. Never post any of your passwords to any Facebook group or page.
- **Facebook:** Use Facebook's Privacy Shortcuts to control your privacy and security on Facebook.
- **Facebook:** Facebook is one of the safest social media platforms to use, but you should have a good understanding of how to use Facebook and its features in

order to use it safely. If you need some training on using Facebook, visit www.infinityguides.com and watch the Facebook for Beginners course.

- **Twitter:** There are many online trolls on Twitter. Use the block function frequently and indiscriminately when you come across trolls who target you.
- **Twitter:** Customize your Twitter Safety features in Settings to fit your needs.
- Always use caution when someone you do not know contacts you through a direct message on Instagram or any social media platform.
- **Instagram:** If you have children who use Instagram, read the Instagram section in Chapter 5 about the different type of threats they are prone to.
- **Snapchat:** Always remember the #1 Rule of Social Media when using Snapchat. Everything you send or say on Snapchat could potentially become public, and there is no foolproof way to guarantee that what you send remains completely private.

MOBILE DEVICE

- You should use two-factor authentication if you want an additional layer of security on accounts that contain sensitive information, such as your online bank account. If you are a public figure, you should most definitely use two-factor authentication on all of your accounts, especially your social media accounts.
- Never reply to an automated text message with any sensitive information, including your username, password, or credit card information.
- Never click on a link inside an automated text message that is warning you about a potential security breach unless you were expecting to receive that text message.
- Treat any automated text message you receive from a regular phone number as suspicious if you did not expect to receive it.
- If someone contacts you claiming to be your bank and requests sensitive information, you should verify their identity by asking them to tell you about other recent transactions you have made. If you are still suspicious about the call or unsatisfied with their answers, hang up and call the phone number on the back of your credit or debit card.
- NEVER throw away paper financial statements you receive in the mail. Identity thieves try to steal these from people's trash and then use the statements against them (an identity thief who stole your thrown out bank statements may be able to answer your question about your recent transactions). Instead, you

should always shred your paper statements rather than throwing them in the trash.

- You should never give out your social security number to a person over the phone <u>who called you</u> UNLESS you were expecting to receive that phone call.
- Using an app or service that encrypts your messages is a very good idea. These services basically make it impossible for anyone to hack or access your messages, unless they somehow got access to your device itself. Therefore, you should always make sure you have security enabled on your device.
- You should absolutely use access (lock screen) security on your smartphone, which will protect all of its data including your text messages from intrusion if your device were to ever fall in the wrong hands. The best access security is a lock screen passcode, and it should be at least 6 digits long and not easily guessable.

COMPUTER

- You should purchase and use virus protection software for your computer, as it will provide you with the best possible defense against online threats. Make sure you purchase software from a well-known company and make sure it includes real-time protection, email security, and a firewall.
- Nearly every computer allows you to update your computer automatically, and you should enable this to make sure your computer is always up to date.
- You should use an automatic cloud backup system on your computer if you have any important files on it, such as documents, photos, or videos. Automatic backup is a very easy and secure way to keep your files safe from hard drive crashes, and it also allows you to easily transfer your files to a new computer if needed.

PARENTS AND PARENTAL CONTROLS

- Know and understand the #1 Rule of Social Media, and make sure your children also know and understand it. This #1 Rule provides the basis for all of social media safety and much of internet safety.
- Education and prevention are the two main principles of keeping your children safe while using the internet. Education involves educating yourself and your children on the various risks of online safety and prevention involves taking active steps to prevent your children from harmful content and online activity.
- Start making use of parental controls right away!

- Keep up with the online trends of young people, as they are often changing.
- Know the different risks children are often exposed online. Teenagers are often targeted by online predators and scammers, areas with young children you want to make sure they do not stumble across harmful content.

PASSWORDS

- If one of your online accounts or passwords is stolen compromised, change the password for that account and any other account that uses that password.
- Create a unique universal password that you will easily remember. This will be your standard password, and use variations of this password as outlined in Chapter 11.
- Create a digital or paper document where you will record and keep all of your passwords.
- If you have more than 3 online accounts, then you should not use the same password for all of these accounts.
- Make use of password remembrance tools on devices and browsers.
- Never use easily guessable passwords or passwords that can be easily identified to you.
- Never share your online passwords with anyone through any medium.
- Create a secondary password unrelated to your standard password that you will only use on websites you consider untrustworthy.

CRAIGSLIST OR OTHER CLASSIFIEDS WEBSITES

- If you are going to meet a stranger from Craigslist for transaction, meet in a safe, public place with security cameras.
- If buying or selling something from a Craigslist stranger, agree on a price before you meet
- Never pay for an item until you meet in person, and only pay in cash or through a payment app
- When buying an item, always inspect an item thoroughly before finalizing the transaction
- Always put your safety first when communicating or meeting with someone on Craigslist

Index

A

Acronyms *169*
Ad Blockers *20*
   recommendations *21*
Address
   sharing online *30*
Advertisements *19, 21*
Adware *108*
Amazon Pay *37*
Android *90*
   parental controls *137*
App Privacy *102*
Automatic Cloud Backup *110*

B

Best Practices definition *13*
Brave *15, 91*
Bump *161*

C

Child & Teenager Safety *119*
Chrome *15, 91*
Chromebook *107*
Clickbait *28*
   examples *28*
Computer Safety *107*
   automatic cloud backup *110*
   cleaning *111*
   comparing computers *107*
   computer updates *110*
   malicious software *108*
   parental controls *126*
   recommended apps *112*
   software add-ons *111*
   tips *111*
   video player *112*

   virus protection *109*
Cookies *163*
Craigslist *155*
   being prepared *156*
   buying or selling *158*
   communicating *156*
   email relay *156*
   meeting strangers *158*
   paying *158*
   texting *156*
Credit Card Info Stolen *143, 146*
Cryptocurrency *165*

D

Digital World *14*
Do Not Call Registry *99*
Domains *51*
   checking accuracy *51*

E

Email *41*
   active protection *109*
   attachments *52*
   built-in safety *41*
   checking links *50*
   common scams *53*
   from address *56*
   internet service provider *58*
   more best practices *56*
   naming conventions *57*
   newsletters *45*
   phishing attacks *47*
   recommended providers *58*
   sharing your email address *30*
   spam and junk mail *41*
   unsubscribing *45*
Expectations *14*

F

Facebook *64, 120*
    activity log *74*
    best practices *67*
    common scams.. *64*
    for parents... *121*
    friend requests *64, 66*
    privacy *68*
    private messages.. *67*
    secret conversations *67*
    two-factor authentication *73*
Fake News.. *27*
    identifying *27*
Financial Information
    sharing online *30*
Fire Tablets *90*
Firewall *109*

G

Google Pay... *37*
Government Websites............................... *31*
Grammar Rules *160*

H

Hacked *144*

I

iMessage.. *89*
Infinity Guides.. *167*
Instagram.. *80, 120*
    best practices *83*
    direct messages... *82*
    for parents... *121*
    profile, followers, & following........................ *81*
    safety features... *82*
    scams... *82*
iPad.. *89*
    parental controls *135*
iPhone.. *89*
    parental controls *135*
    privacy *101*

J

Jargon... *160*
Joe Malacina
    about *5*
    books *5*
Junk Mail
    how to deal with it.. *44*
    recognizing.. *42*

K

Key Terms *13*
Kindle *90*

L

Linux Computer.. *107*
Location Privacy *103*

M

Mac *107*
Malware.. *108*
Match.com *113*
Memes *160*
Microsoft Edge.................................... *15, 91*
Mobile Device Safety *89*
    Amazon.. *90*
    Apple.. *89*
    Google *90*
    privacy *91, 101*
    private browsing *91*
    Samsung *90*
    securing your devices *102*
    texting & messaging *92*
    web browsers *91*
    web browsing *91*
More Resources *167*
Mozilla Firefox.................................... *15, 91*

N

Name

sharing online 30
Noob 161
Number Neighbors 98

O

Off The Grid 161
OKCupid 114
Online Dating...113
   background checks 116
   investigating profiles 116
   meeting 117
   pay-to-play scams......................................115
   platforms 113
   protecting yourself 114
   verification scams 115
   viewing profiles 115
Online definition 13
Online Identity 57
Online Safety
   definition 13
Online Shopping Safety 33
   1st rule 33
   2nd rule 36
   how to pay 36
   paying 35
   providing information 35
   receipts..38
   third-party payers.......................................37
   tips..40
   trusting websites 38
   you've been scammed.................................144

P

Parental Controls..119
   #1 Rule of Social media 119
   activity reports 127
   Android devices..137
   app limits...130
   best practices 140
   built-in tools 140
   child email addresses 139
   computers 126
   content filters.....................................127, 130
   definition 125
   Downtime...130

   education..119
   Facebook risks 121
   financial data protection 139
   Instagram risks 121
   iPhone or iPad..135
   location tracking 127
   Mac computer 127
   other online risks 125
   other social media risks 124
   screen time 127
   smartphones & tablets 135
   Snapchat risks 123
   social media platforms................................120
   social media risks 121
   software..139
   teen acronyms 142
   teen apps 141
   Twitter risks 124
   what kids are using 120
   Windows PC..126
Password Hacked 147
Passwords 149
   creating a standard.....................................149
   disclosing 155
   PINs..154
   secondary password 155
   storing..150, 153
PayPal...37
Personal Information
   sharing online 29
Phishing Emails 47
Phone Calls..99
   common scams 99
Phone Number
   sharing 30
Pinterest...120
Pixel Smartphone...90
Plenty of Fish..114
Premium Snapchat..86

R

Ransomware 108, 145
Referral Content 21
   examples..24
   free information 21
   paid referrals 21

179

S

Safari 15, 91
Shopping Safety 33
Silk Web Browser 91
Smartphones .... *See* Mobile Device Safety
   definition 13
Snapchat 83, 120
   best practices 86
   for parents 123
   friends 85
   private messages 85
   risks 86
   sexually explicit content 86
   snap definition 84
   warnings 84
Social Media 61
   #1 Rule 61
   account history 88
   being harassed 145
   best practices 87
   definition 13
   if your account was hacked 145
   naming conventions 87
   privacy 62, 63
   private messages 62
Social Security Number 31
Sponsored Content 24
   example 25
   markers 26
Spyware 108
SSL Security 33
   checking 33

T

Tablets .... *See* Mobile Device Safety
   definition 13
Telemarketing 99
Text Messaging 92
   automated texts 93
   links 96
   privacy 101
   scams 96
Third-Party Payers 37
TikTok 120

Tinder 113
Top Level Domain 31
Trolls 63, 161
   identifying 63
Tumblr 120
Twitter 75, 120
   best practices 80
   blocking profiles 80
   common scams 77
   direct messages 76
   followers 75
   following profiles 75
   for parents 124
   hiding sensitive content 79
   links 76
   muting profiles 80
   private account 79
   safety features 78
   tweets 76
   warnings 75
Two-Factor Authentication 93

V

Victim of Phishing Attack 144
Viruses 108
   infected 144
   mobile devices 109
   protection software 109
   real-time protection 109
VPNs - Virtual Private Networks 162

W

Web Browser
   recommendations 15
Web Browsing 15
   advertisements 19
   data collection 16
   privacy concerns 16
   privacy policy 19
   private browsing 16
Webcam Security 111
WhatsApp 102
Windows PC 107

Check out more beginner's guides and manuals at:

www.infinityguides.com